FLOWERS
Growing · Drying · Preserving

FLOWERS
Growing · Drying · Preserving

Alan Cormack and David Carter

CRESCENT BOOKS
NEW YORK

Stamen (Service through agriculture for the mentally handicapped) was founded by David Carter and his wife Ann to provide advice about the use of agriculture and horticulture as a base for training, education, occupation and employment for people with mental handicap. Stamen offers professional advice to local authorities, voluntary agencies, government departments and private individuals. Many rural projects for disabled people through Britain and Ireland owe their existence to the work of Stamen. The search for horticultural activities suitable for the handicapped led to David's professional interest in the cultivation of plant material for preservation. Alan Cormack joined Stamen to research methods of drying and preserving plant material. Their separate approaches to this fascinating subject resulted in their authorship of this book.

Special thanks to Jane Newdick for her chapter on Flower Arranging; to Daan Hogewoning, jr. of W. Hogewoning BV, Holland, for allowing us to use their pictures (credited at the end of this book) and for their kindness and advice; to Ingrid van der Marel of the Bloemenbureau, Holland, for the use of their pictures of Dutch produced flowers courtesy of the Flower Council, Holland; and to Mary Fahy for her demonstrations of step by step flower arranging.

Executive Managers   Kelly Flynn
Susan Egerton-Jones
Art Editor   Julie Williamson
Editorial Assistant   Fiona Thomas
Production   Peter Phillips

1987 Edition published by Crescent Books,
distributed by Crown Publishers, Inc.
Edited and designed by the
Artists House Division of
Mitchell Beazley International Ltd
Artists House
14–15 Manette Street
London W1V 5LB
An Artists House Book
© Mitchell Beazley Publishers 1987
Reprinted 1988

ISBN 0-517-61204-6

Typeset by Hourds Typographica, Stafford.
Reproduction by La Cromolito s.n.c., Milan.
Printed in Portugal by Printer Portuguesa Industria Grafica Lda.

CONTENTS

INTRODUCTION

There are several ways of preserving "dried" flowers and people who take up this hobby for the first time have many different expectations of what a dried flower should look like. What some regard as beautiful, others will dislike. Some will be looking for a single perfectly shaped rose, as near in colour to the original as possible. Others will want a mass of colour and texture to act as the bulk of a flower arrangement. Some will want scent and others foliage. And their gardens, too, will differ in their suitability for growing different species: sheltered and sunny on rich alluvial soil, or blasted by salt spray on a cliff top. The white "Bells of Ireland" may represent their perfect dried flower, while others will prefer bright red dyed grasses.

We all tend to hope for a perfect, everlasting beauty, but it does not exist. Only the artificial silk blossoms that grace the tables of certain restaurants, and, rather surprisingly, the shelves of some garden centres, can begin to reach this kind of perfection. Those for whom even the slightest flaw is a deficiency will be happy with silk flowers on their tables all winter, but for those who like a plant closer to the original, with its vigour and all its blemishes, this book will be more useful.

Having decided that you will be happy with blemishes, that you don't want silken perfection, ponder for a moment. Whatever you do to a flower will alter it somewhat. So you may as well resolve to alter it in the way you want. Try to make use of any defects. Towards the end of this book is a section on flower arranging that shows you how to use

different species, in a variety of combinations and for many tastes and effects. But you don't have to follow it. If you want to alter all the guidelines that are given here, of course you can, and the chances are you will – after a bit of practice – achieve exactly what you want.

And the same goes for flower drying. To start you off on this fascinating hobby, we have given descriptions of certain standard methods, which if followed ought to provide you with a certain level of success in most cases. We hope that to have examples to follow, and ideas to dig into, will help you cultivate your own experience. But please don't follow these ideas slavishly. For one thing your own needs and intentions will vary. I know a retired professor, originally interested in preserving biological material, who embeds large seedheads of dandelions in the middle of globes of clear plastic, and gives them to his friends. I also know a charity that sells heads of Molucella by the thousand.

There's only one way to find out what you want to do, and that's by experiment. By all means use our advice as a starting point. But don't stick to it. Swap methods. Swap mixtures. Try different arrangements and different species. And think about your own particular preferences. In the end, if you do this, you will enjoy not only the finished object, the dried flower, whether a single, perfectly dried rose, in a glass case, or a bunch of mixed species, acting as an altarpiece, or on a sideboard, but also you will have enjoyed the process. Enjoy discovering what it is that makes your preferences. Enjoy your skills and your abilities. Then I hope you will also enjoy this book, which is going to act as a jumping off point for so many evenings' activity.

Good luck with your flowers!

IDENTIFICATION CATALOGUE

There are a large number of flowers that are suitable for drying; some are quite exotic, some can be grown easily outdoors, others need a bit of pampering and special conditions. We have selected here species and varieties that are, generally, available to gardeners – though in some cases they may need hunting down – and that can be grown successfully at home by all enthusiasts. This is not a definitive list, and keen home dryers should experiment with other species. But here, we hope, the information given on what the dried or growing plants look like and how to grow, harvest and dry them will prove both an inspiration and a practical base for experiment.

Acacia spp.   WATTLES
Leguminosae

Achillea millefolium   YARROW
Compositae

This genus is a native of Australia, where it is very common. It has bright yellow flowers arranged in either a ball or a cylinder and in cool regions generally should be grown in a conservatory or greenhouse, although *Acacia dealbata* will survive throughout many temperature areas if sheltered.

If, under glass, the trees or shrubs are grown in containers, it may be possible to lift them out into the summer sunshine.

Two of those we have chosen show the characteristic bipinnate leaves of the genus. The leaves are divided into leaflets on either side of a central stem, and these leaflets are then subdivided into smaller leaflets.

Acacia longifolia – SYDNEY GOLDEN WATTLE – is the odd one out. Instead of leaves, it has phyllodes or flattened, pointed, tapering, green stems. Its flower heads are arranged in yellow cylinders at the base of these. This species is hardy in mild regions, but elsewhere is best grown in a cool greenhouse.

Acacia baileyana – COOTAMUNDA WATTLE – is another species that needs the same amount of warmth as *Acacia longifolia*. It has spherical, bright yellow flower heads, arranged on slender dropping branches, and bipinnate leaves.

Acacia dealbata – SILVER WATTLE – is hardier and has been grown outdoors in some temperature regions. It dislikes lime, and has sweet-scented yellow flowers that often go under the name of "Mimosa".

To dry the Acacias, it's normally enough to hang their flowers in a warm moving airstream. Although we have not done so ourselves, we think a worthwhile experiment would be to try preserving a whole stem in a glycerine-water mixture. This ought to make the flowers more attractive and keep the foliage green and glossy.

What an appropriate name for this little plant that grows about 30cm (12in) tall and is found on so many patches of wasteland! It has a long medicinal history as a plant whose leaves can be crushed, perhaps by chewing, and applied to wounds. It is an easy and attractive plant to dry, especially the more colourful cultivated species. The name "millefolium" means "thousand-leaved" and exactly describes the finely divided foliage of the common species. It has a strong smell characteristic of many members of the family and this makes it unpalatable to livestock. Perhaps this is one reason the plant is so common. It also seems resistant to trampling and bruising by hordes of plant dryers.

All the species have flowers arranged in flat heads. In *Achilles millefolium*, the wild species, these are white or pinkish. *Achillea filpendulina* is a larger cultivated plant 0.6–1.5m (2–5ft) tall with bright yellow flowers up to 12.7cm (5in) in diameter. *Achillea ptarmica* has greenish white flowers and undivided leaves with larger, less tightly packed flowerheads, while *Achillea millefolium rosea* (Cerise Queen) is a cultivated variety of the wild species.

If you decide to grow the plant instead of picking it from the wild, it needs well-drained soil, perhaps with some sand in it, and a sunny position. Sow the seeds where you want them to grow in spring, or split the roots and transplant them in spring or autumn.

The plant can be dried quite easily by being cut and tied in bunches, which are then hung in the roof of the potting shed or in an indoor drying cupboard as suggested in the section on air-drying. *Achillea filpendulina* holds its colour well to give masses of vivid yellow flowerheads.

A. PTARMICA

A. FILIPENDULINA

Ageratum houstonianum
AGERATUM
Compositae

The flower's genetic name – a geratum, means "not ageing". It would be nice to think this referred to the plant's suitability for drying. Originally a native of Mexico, as shown by its alternative Latin name, *Ageratum mexicanum,* nowadays it has been bred to give more compact, hence more useful plants, which are suitable for bedding. They can also be grown in the greenhouse to give show specimens.

This is a half-hardy annual specimen, 46cm (18in) to maybe 0.6m (2ft) high with blue or white and occasionally pink flowers. It likes well-drained fertile soil and should be planted out after it has been hardened off in a cold frame.

Sow the seeds at the end of winter over heat, in a temperature of 16–18°C (60–65°F). The seedlings should be kept at 10–13°C (50–55°F) night, temperature 16–18°C (60–65°F day) until they are large enough to prick out into boxes or small pots, depending upon the use for which they are intended. They can be sown in the autumn and kept through the winter in a heated greenhouse. In either case the plants should be pinched back to ensure compact growth and, if they are being grown for the winter, care should be taken not to water them too freely. It is possible to take cuttings of them, using soft material and putting it into a light compost over heat.

Ageratum could be dried in a drying medium, but the rather fluffy flowers make it difficult to remove the silica gel from between the petals, unless you shake and brush them vigorously, which tends to damage the flower. On the whole, the best way is probably in warm moving air, hung head downwards in bunches. The bright blue varieties tend to look particularly attractive.

Alchemilla sp.
LADY'S MANTLE
Rosaceae

Allium spp.
ONIONS
Liliaceae

A. MOLLIS

A. ALFATUENSE

AIR DRIED

The old alchemists believed that *Alchemilla vulgaris* could be used to convert lead into gold. So its Latin specific name is an Arabic word for alchemy.

It is an easily grown but slightly dull species, with small yellow-green flowers that have no petals, and the advantage of being hardy. It's mainly a wild flower, though it is grown in gardens for its somewhat spreading form and attractively lobed leaves.

If you grow it, rather than picking – with discretion – from the wild, it can be given an early start by being sown in a cold greenhouse in mid-spring, and planted out later. Alternatively, sow it where it is to be grown and be prepared to keep it in check, because it can take over, particularly in a rock garden.

Our illustration shows another, more showy species, *Alchemilla mollis*, which would also be worth drying.

Try drying the leaves in a current of air, or for fun, you might try pressing it, placing its leaves between pads of white blotting paper, or newspaper faced with blotting paper for economy. Place these bundles of paper between hardboard and put weights on them. Old flat irons are the best thing, but small boulders, bricks or piles of scrap iron will do as well. You can use one piece of board and another flat surface such as a table. Change the paper fairly often to make sure the plants dry properly, and when they are ready, try glueing them in patterns on sheets of coloured cardboard, perhaps with drawn or painted designs to go with them.

A. KARATAVIENSE

A. GIGANTEUM

Human beings have been eating the onion bulb for several thousand years, and it has been used as a herbal antiseptic and in homeopathic medicine. For arranging its shapely and colourful flowerheads, which can be obtained in many shades of blue, lilac, yellow and white, there are literally dozens of species, and we have somewhat arbitrarily chosen a few of them. All have more or less spherical flower heads made up of many individual florets whose stems are set radially over the surface.

One word of warning. The whole onion plant has a strong smell. The bulbs are well-known for making cooks cry and the scent may be quite objectionable to flower arrangers with sensitive noses. If you feel like this about them, we suggest that you try different species until you find one whose smell is weak enough not to offend you; its strength does vary widely between species.

All species may be propagated by bulbils, or by seed (except in the case of *A. albiosum* and *A. karataviense* which do not breed true). Seed should be less than about two years old, to retain its vitality, and should be sown in drills 25–30cm (10–12in) apart, and lightly covered. If flower production falls off after the second year, the plant should be dug up and divided.

Onions should be grown in sunny situations on rich loam, but can be grown on any soil.

They can be dried in a moving current of warm air, although this can cause some shrivelling and you may be better off using silica gel if you want perfect specimens.

Here are some species which you may like to grow

A. aflatuense		Purple-lilac flowers 4″ diam.	0.9m (2½ft)
A. albopilosum	STAR OF PERSIA	Lilac flowers	1m (3ft) high
A. caeruleum (= *A. azureum*)	BLUE GLOBE ONION	Blue flowers	0.6–1.2m (2–4ft) high
A. giganteum	GIANT ONION	Blue to purple flowers	1–2m high
A. karataviense	TURKESTAN ONION	Whitish flowers	1.2m
A. moly	LILY LEEK OR GOLDEN GARLIC	Yellow flowers	0.4m (1½ft) high
A. rosenbachianum	ROSEṄBACH ONION	Rose purple flowers	1.2m (4ft) high

Amaranthus caudatus
LOVE-LIES-BLEEDING
Amaranthaceae

Ammobium alatum
WINGED EVERLASTING
Compositae

Flower dryers keep meeting plants whose names have to do with the flowers lasting forever. This decorative art seems to have a long history, although the Greeks appear to have dried their flowers for rather different purposes from modern-day arrangers. *Amaranthus*, for instance, is supposed to have been used for tomb decoration.

The drooping heads look like blood clots and this leads to their popular name "Love-Lies-Bleeding".

There are several related species of *Amaranthus caudatus*. The traditional one grows up to three feet tall and has long red drooping flower spikes. *Amaranthus hypochondriacus* has upright red spikes and several others such as *Amaranthus tricolor* also have brightly variegated leaves.

All these species should be sown under glass at 21°C (70°F) in mid-spring, thinned, then planted out about a month later into good rich loamy soil. They need full sun and good drainage and can be grown in large pots in a greenhouse at 15°C (60°F) to produce showy specimens.

For drying, pick the flower spikes as soon as they open or you may find that you lose some of the florets. Dry them in warm moving air, or if you have an especially treasured specimen try it on its side in a long shallow container of silica gel. If you do so, be sure to brush the powder from between the flowers after the spike has finished drying.

The generic name of this plant means "living in sand" which gives you some idea of the kind of conditions that suit it under cultivation. It's a member of the daisy family, whose ray florets have been replaced by a dense ring of dry white bracts, which look somewhat like petals. The disc florets are yellow, in the centre of the flowerheads, and somewhat less important when the flower has been dried. The specific name is the Latin word meaning "winged" and describes the flattened angles to the stems. Its English name is also descriptive.

There is a variety *Ammobium alatum grandiflorum* whose flowers are about 5cm (2in) in diameter as opposed to half this size or less for the normal plant, and it would be wll worth growing this if you can get hold of its seed. However, the ordinary plant is frequently dried successfully. It grows about 1m (3ft) high, likes a well-drained soil, and plenty of sun. Seeds can be sown either under glass in early spring and the seedlings planted out after danger of frost is over, or the plant may be sown indoors in September and overwintered under glass. The plants are ready for growing on in the following spring, and are larger, stronger specimens than can be grown as annuals.

This genus is easy to dry. Don't allow the flowers to mature too far, cut them, tie them in bunches, and hang these up in a current of warm moving air. It would also be a good subject for dyeing by total immersion (the "dunkit") method. See *Preserving with glycerine* section for more details.

Anaphalis margaritacea
PEARLY EVERLASTING
Compositae

Anetheum graveolens
DILL
Umbelliferae

These are flowers of the Daisy family, but unlike the flowers of the Common Daisy which has disc florets in the centre and flat white ray florets around the edge of its inflorescence, this genus has only disc florets. These are greyish to pearly white, and form dense flat heads up to 12cm (5in) across above woolly stems and grey-green leaves.

It's a hardy perennial that can easily be grown from seed, sown in mid-spring, in a cold frame or can be divided in autumn. *Anaphalis* likes a well-drained sunny part of the garden.

Air drying is the best for it, indeed any other kind of drying would be wasted, and it's also a good plan to try dyeing. This can give some variety to its rather uniform silvery appearance. Choose several different colours, perhaps red, turquoise and blue for example, and dry a few specimens of the dried flowers in each of them to give a more interesting bouquet. The best way to do this is to lay the flowers in a flat container and submerge them in dye until they have reached a suitable intensity of colour. Then take them out, drain them, and allow them to dry again. Take care while you are doing this not to damage the flowerheads, especially during the second drying.

Also called *Peucadanum graveolens*, the name "Dill" comes from the Old Norse "dilla" "to lull", and when I discovered this I thought that this plant must have been used to make people drowsy. The herbals, however, list it as a "carminative" – a plant to relieve flatulence.

In fact it's a pleasant smelling plant, up to some 1m (3ft) high with small yellow flowers, which can be grown as a biennial or an annual, although it does not always produce flowers in its first year. The seed should be drilled 30–60cm (2–3ft) apart and the plants thinned to about 46cm (18in) in order to encourage flower development. Closer spacings are all right for foliage. Ordinary soil suits it quite well but it does like sunshine.

Pick the stems well before any seeds have developed, and hang them head down in bunches in a stream of warm moving air, until they have dried thoroughly. When they are grown for medical purposes, the heads are allowed to ripen, then dried so that the seeds can be thrashed and essential oil extracted from them. The seeds are also used with fish and pickled cucumber to give them a distinctive aromatic flavour.

Asclepias syriaca
SILK WEED
Asclepiaceae

Astilbe sp.
GOATSBEARD
Saxafrigaceae

This is sometimes known as Ipecacuanha but should not be confused with the drug Ipecacuanha (generally used as an emetic for children) which comes from a plant called BRAZIL ROOT (whose Latin name is *Cephaelis ipecahuanha*).

Asclepias syriaca has been used as an asthma remedy and the down produced round the seeds has been woven into materials and used as a stuffing for pillows. It has also been used to make fine soft-haired brooms once employed for sweeping away fleas from the floors of rooms.

In America the plant is a common wildflower but it is normally cultivated in Europe.

It has green to purple sweet-smelling flowers in umbels that are about 5cm (2in) in diameter. It is hardy (and a perennial) but does like a sunny situation and peaty soil. It is not lime or clay tolerant. In the first place, try growing the plant from seed or find a friend who has it and beg some divisions from them. This can be done in the early spring, which is also a good time to sow seed, although plants can be grown later than this and overwintered.

There are a number of greenhouse species, of which we suggest you try *Asclepias curassavica* (BLOODFLOWER). This needs a minimum temperature of 18°C (65°F) and should be grown in a pot in the greenhouse, being kept slightly dry overwinter before being cut back and repotted. It has bright orange and red flowers.

Both these species can be dried in a current of warm moving air, though it might also be worthwhile trying them with silica gel.

A hardy herbaceous perennial with feathery, plume-like pointed heads of tiny, pink to red or white flowers, rising above a clump of deeply divided, pointed leaves. There are a number of different species, which vary in their leaf shape, and the shape and colour of the flower heads.

Astilbe is most satisfactorily propagated by division, but seed may be sown under glass in spring, and planted out later. The plants are best divided in spring. *Astilbe* likes loamy soil and plenty of water, so is good for growing by ponds, and does well whether in shaded or sunny borders. It needs watering in dry weather. The plants can be readily forced, in pots, in a coolish greenhouse.

Cut the flowers with plenty of stem, and hang them upside down to dry individually, in the dark, in a current of warm dry air.

Banksia spp.

BANKSIA
Proteaceae

B. COCCINEA

B. SPINOSA

These plants are as worthwhile growing for their foliage as for their fruit clusters. The trouble is that you may have difficulty finding specimens of either because they are difficult to grow and need cool greenhouse conditions. Since they are trees or shrubs, you need either a rather large greenhouse or a deep pocket to afford the imported seed heads (usually from Australia or South Africa) which are the commercial arranger's usual source of material.

Both species are adapted to life in a dry climate and are named after Sir Joseph Banks, one of the world's great plant hunters and botanist's.

Banksia coccinea is up to 4.5m (15ft) tall, with evergreen prickly toothed leaves and vertically ribbed flower heads up to 8cm (3in) in diameter. Its flowers have white bases and scarlet tips.

Banksia baxterii is a slightly smaller shrub with leathery, broadly triangular leaves and spherical flowerheads.

They both need well drained, dryish acid soil, such as a mixture of loam and peat, with some silver sand, and fresh seed must be used if they are propagated in this way because otherwise it loses its viability. It is probably better to propagate by cuttings, if you can find a tree to take them from in the first place. Neither trees nor cuttings should be allowed to wilt.

Generally the seed heads are the parts most used in flower arranging, and these can be air dried.

Calendula officinalis COMMON MARIGOLD
Compositae

Calluna vulgaris LING
Ericaceae

C. VULGARIS 'SILVER KNIGHT'

This member of the Compositae, unlike *Anaphalis*, has both kinds of florets, a dense mass of disc florets in the centre of its flowers and one or more rings of ray florets around the edges. The colour varies from orange to yellow, often with differences between the different kinds of florets and it is one of the best known garden species, usually growing about 30cm (1ft) tall and being rather untidy.

It's been known for hundreds of years as a herb used in cooking, colouring cheese and for strengthening the heart. It's Latin name means "the first day of the month", probably a reference to the fact that in some areas the flower blooms all the year round, while its English name refers to the Virgin Mary – "Mary's Gold".

It's a native of the Mediterranean region, but grows like a weed elsewhere – once you have it in your garden you may have difficulty getting rid of it. Just scatter the seed in a drill in mid-spring and thin to about 25cm (9in). It is possible to grow earlier specimens by starting the seed under light heat in the greenhouse. Do not grow them in rich soil because the plants may become rather leggy and not produce the most showy blossoms.

The summer specimens are the best ones to dry, because early or late blooms can be rather gappy and lopsided. Although people do dry them by hanging them up in a moving airstream I feel the plants deserve rather better than this. Just because they're so common and easily grown, that's no reason not to make the most of them. I would dry them head down on silica gel, carefully covering the back of the flower with the same medium and brushing it gently from between the ray florets when they have dried properly.

The Latin name comes from the Greek *calluna*, "to cleanse" because it was once used as a broom. The proper English name is "Ling", although the plant is often called "Heather". This name should be reserved for plants of the genus *Erica* which differ from the present genus in having a green calyx and short lobes on the corolla. *Calluna* has a deeply lobed corolla, and its calyx is not only the same colour as the petals, but longer. Both are pale purple and together form long thin spikes of pointed-looking flowers, unlike the more rounded clusters of the bell-shaped heather flowers.

"Heather" is an important honey plant, and in the past has had a number of practical uses, such as broom-making, thatching for cottages and providing springy bedding. It is still a most important food plant for grouse and grows in large quantities on the moorlands of Britain where it is burnt in rotation to ensure a supply of fresh growth for the birds.

It likes poor acid soils with plenty of peat or even coarse sand because these simulate its wild habitat. It does not need fertilizers and is not tolerant of lime. Straggly specimens can be clipped to make them grow more bushy.

"Heather" is an extremely easy plant to dry. At one time people returning home from holidays in Scotland carried bunches of it tied to the fronts of their cars and later transferred it to jam jars in the kitchen. In fact, the flowers will dry on the plant to some extent, and will certainly dry in a vase with no water! However, they will keep their colour and quality better if they are hung in an airy dark place, to prevent bleaching.

Celosia cristata   COCKSCOMB
Amaranthaceae

Centaurea cyanus   CORNFLOWER
Compositae

The name of this plant literally means "the crested burnt flower". It's a tender annual, native of tropical Asia, with fused, globular, fanlike, dark red, yellow, crimson or scarlet flowers. Celosias are tropical plants which have long been grown as conservatory annuals. The cockscomb has flattened fused fan like flower heads whereas the Prince of Wales Feather varieties – *C. Pyramidalis* – have pyramid-shaped feathery flowers.

Celosias have to be grown rapidly and well to produce large heads for drying. Pot or bed cultivation under glass or polythene is needed with seedlings being raised in heat in early spring. They grow best in good light conditions and should never be allowed to get dry at the roots. Good "combs" should be 22–30cm (9–12in) long, 8–15cm (3–6in) wide on plants which are 15–22cm (6–9in) high.

The flower should be dried with care. Cut the blooms with plenty of stem and strip off the leaves from the lower part beneath the stems. Make yourself a number of long boxes, out of stout card, taped together at the edges with masking tape. About two-thirds of the way up, tape in a piece of stiff wire mesh of an appropriate size to fit the box's cross-section. This should be large enough to accommodate the flower head held vertically. Cover the mesh with strong paper. Then make a hole in the paper and push the stem of the Cockscomb through it.

Sprinkle silica gel carefully around the flower, making sure that it covers the underside completely. Add more silica gel, then tap again. When the flower is nicely embedded in the agent, begin to sprinkle silica gel carefully over its upper surface until it is completely covered. If the boxes are rather tall, they can be taped together in groups of six. When the flowers have dried, follow the instructions for inspecting and uncovering them given on p.74.

This used to be an abundant weed of cornfields but its commonness has greatly decreased because of the extensive use of modern selective herbicides which kill broadleaved weeds while leaving the narrow-leaved cereals. For many of us this is a source of sorrow at the loss of brilliant colours from the countryside, yet the old time reaper would have been glad of the benefits of herbicides because this plant's hard stem was such a nuisance in blunting the sickle that it was given the name of Hurt Sickle.

It may still be possible to find wild specimens of the "Bluebottle", as it is also called, along the bottoms of hedges or in batches of less cultivated land. It can be recognized by its bright blue spreading florets with lobed tips, around a more purple central head, and by the leaves, which are narrow and greyish with long lobes near the bottom of the plant and no lobes at all higher up.

The juice of the flowers has been used for blue ink and for dyeing. In neither case is the colouring permanent, so the flowers may be expected to fade in dried arrangements.

If you have trouble finding the wild variety, remember that it has been bred extensively since Elizabethan times, to give cultivars a wider choice of white, pink and reddish flowers, as well as the more common "cornflower blue" variety. These plants are usually rather taller, perhaps because of the more cosseted conditions under which they're grown and may provide the materials for more impressive arrangements.

As may be expected of a weed, the flower needs no special growing arrangements beyond seed sprinkled in ordinary garden soil, and thinning to about 38cm (15in).

It is easy to dry in a current of warm moving air.

Cotinus coggynia atropurpurea

PURPLE SMOKE TREE
Anacardiaceae

Also known as *Rhus continus*, the English name of the tree is suggested by the thread-like stalks of the flowers, which give it the effect of being surrounded by smoke. Different varieties have been bred by horticulturists to have various pinkish or purplish flowers and sometimes similar colours in their leaves. This one is sometimes also called "The Venetian Suimach" or "Burning Bush" and is a very striking tree. You should grow one of the "smoke" varieties to obtain the maximum impact from it.

Propagate by soft cuttings, preferably using a hormone rooting compound. Or it can be grown from seed, but seeds need three months in warm conditions – for example, inside your airing cupboard – and another three months at a cooler temperature before they will germinate. The tree needs full sun and dryish poorish soils, and likes quite a lot of attention and water for the first few years. After that it will flower on its own.

Try drying the mass of pinkish "smoke" simply by keeping the twigs in moving air in a dark place. Of if you want to experiment, use glycerine, or better still glycol, or perhaps a touch of reddish or purplish florists dye first, in water, to try and intensify the purplish colours. The foliage is also a beautiful purple colour and you may want to preserve it using glycerine or glycol.

Craspedia uniflora
CRASPEDIA
Compositae

Cucurbita pepo-ovifea
GOURDS
Cucurbitaceae

These flowers of the Daisy family have no strap-shaped ray florets like those found on the edges of Daisies. Instead their flowers are composed entirely of white or yellow disc florets, gathered together in round-topped heads about 3cm (1in) in diameter.

Although in their native country of New Zealand they are perennials, in Britain they are usually cultivated as annuals, being sown in the greenhouse and planted out when frost danger is over. They like a well drained soil, plenty of sun, and grow to about 30cm (12in) high.

They are easy to dry, the heads being cut with long stems, tied in bunches and hung head downwards in a dry, moving airstream.

This plant has long rambling stems with tendrils and produces gourds in a variety of shapes and colours. Buy a mixture of strains, at least at first, to find out which ones you prefer, and to add variety to your arranging.

Sow the seeds under glass in late spring. If cloches are used the soil must be warmed for at least 10 days before sowing, or pots can be used in the greenhouse or cold frame. Both seeds and mature plants like a rich soil so compost should be added to the pots and plenty of compost or manure should be forked into the spot where they are to be transplanted. It's a good idea to grow them on a mound to avoid unnecessary digging and to make sure that the plants have good drainage. They like to have at least their heads in the sun. If the roots are to be shaded, add a little sand to the mounds to make the drainage more free.

The young plants should be kept covered with cloches until they're well established, and the mature plants allowed to ramble over a trellis or sunny bush.

To dry the gourds, place them in a warm dry place – moving air is not necessary – and leave them for a few weeks. Scrub the skins to remove dirt and polish with a good wax polish. Some people recommend cutting a hole near the stem to remove seeds and flesh, and this may be a good idea if you want to carve or varnish them. To remove the thin outer skin, first dip the gourd briefly in boiling water, then rub it with a soft cloth. Do not wax it if you're going to apply varnish because this will not adhere to the waxed surface. Gourds which had been treated like this were traditionally placed in the fireplace when it was no longer needed for winter heating.

Dahlia spp.

DAHLIA
Compositae

AIR DRIED

This plant is named after the Swedish botanist Anders Dahl. It hybridizes extremely easily so horticulturists have bred a vast number of cultivated varieties that do not usually breed true from seed and must be propagated by cuttings, especially for showing.

The cultivation of Dahlias is something of a mystique and it's only possible to mention briefly a very broad outline. Root cuttings in a warm place or divide up existing rootstocks and harden off the young plants before planting them outside in deep rich soils, after all danger of frost is over. Alternatively sow seeds towards the end of winter and risk its not turning out to be quite true to the parent.

Some varieties will not bloom before the autumn frosts and must be brought into the greenhouse in order to do so. Others are allowed to be killed by the frost after they have bloomed and then are lifted and the tubers dried off before being stored in a frost-proof place until next spring.

This is a flower that ought to be dried using silica gel, although it can also be air dried. When using silica gel, take great care to sprinkle the powder evenly between the petals so that it supports them and they retain their original shape. I suggest that you support the flowers on a sheet of cardboard or polystyrene ceiling tile and allow the stems to air-dry underneath it, because they're not too important to the final display. it may be worth stripping any foliage from them before you do this. Alternatively, cut off the head leaving a short length of stem attached to a pin or florist's wire, and mount it on an artificial stem later.

AIR DRIED

Delphinium ajacis   LARKSPUR
Ranunculaceae

Delphinium hybridum   PERENNIAL DELPHINIUM
Ranunculaceae

This is an annual grown for its white, pink, purple and blue flower spikes. It is named after a fanciful resemblance between a lark's "spur" or claw and the pointed spurs found on the backs of the flowers. There is also an annual or biennial plant known as *Delphinium consolida*. Between the two of them they can boast a large number of forms with different colours and flower shapes including double and double-spurred varieties.

Sow them in early spring, in rich soil and at least half-a-day's sunshine, and water them in a dry summer. The taller varieties may need some twiggy support if they are not to be blown over.

Delphinium ajacis in particular dries well and the white varieties are sometimes dyed either by being stood in a container of dye which is then drawn up into the petals, or by being laid flat in a bath of dye after they have already been dried. Although they are air-dried on the stem, some people consider it necessary to remove the flowerheads and dry them on florist's wires or pins, even dyeing them separately before glueing them onto their own or artificial stems. Which you do depends on what sort of arranging you're going to use them for.

There are many different species of hybrid delphiniums and a lazy botanist's way of lumping them together is to use the Latin name. This is one case where it would perhaps be more sensible to use the general English name, though usually botanists don't like to do so because normally the Latin name is more accurate.

It's interesting that the word "Delphinium" comes from the Greek word *delphin*, meaning a dolphin, because of a fancied resemblance between the spurred flower and a dolphin's head. Evidently this genus inspired people with fertile imaginations (see also the origin of name *Delphinium ajacis*).

However, worrying about different varieties or species is all quite irrelevant to a flower drier, because the parts which he or she will use are the seed heads. This is where it is so much easier to be a practical craftsperson than a practising botanist.

The plants are very tall 2–2.5m (6–8ft) and need propagating from cuttings every three or four years if they're to maintain their vigour. Staking is essential. The plants like good soil and often grow to their full height, which makes them susceptible to wind shake. They are sometimes attacked by mildew which can be controlled by a fungicide, applied if necessary throughout the growing season.

Drying could not be easier. Sometimes the seed heads will dry on the plant stems. This shows that they don't need much attention – at most hanging for a while in dry moving air.

Dryandra formosa   Proteaceae

Echinops   GLOBE THISTLE
Compositae

This is an evergreen shrub, related to Banksia, which doesn't appear to have a precise English name. If it does it's probably "Dryandra" because it's customary to transfer the Latin name into English in cases where there's any doubt. It's taken from the name of a Swedish botanist, Joseph Dryander, who was a pupil of Linnaeus and later became Joseph Banks's librarian as well as the first librarian of the Linnaean Society.

The plant has sword-shaped leaves and an orange-yellow flower 5–7.5cm (2–3in) long by 4cm (1½in) wide and must be grown in a cool greenhouse where it needs well-drained, dryish acid soil such as a loam-peat mixture with some coarse sand, and considerable headroom. Although listed as a shrub, it can grow up to 4.5m (15ft) high. It can be stood outside in the summer if grown in a suitable container but you'd need several strong gardeners to move a full-sized specimen.

On the whole we think you would be wiser to buy dried specimens from importers of dried plant material unless you are rather ambitious and happen to have a large greenhouse.

The Latin name of the genus comes from the Greek meaning "like a hedgehog" and indeed the round blue flowerheads with their florets all pointing outwards might be said to resemble this animal.

Echinops exaltatus is a biennial and like most thistles is rough and spiny. The silvery blue colour of its foliage is unusual and well worth drying in itself to add an interesting colour to arrangements. It is a very large species growing up to 3m (10ft) tall, although normally it achieves about half this height. If this is felt to be rather overpowering in a small garden, you could try the perennial species *Echinops ritro* which grows only to about 45cm (12in), has more spherical flowerheads and downy leaves.

Both species will grow well in ordinary garden soil in full sun but the seed must be bought from a reputable supplier, or it may not be true. Even then it is better to propagate the perennial species by division because this gives better colour.

The flowers should be cut just before they are fully open, to make sure that the florets do not shed on drying, and dried head downwards in a warm moving airstream. it might be a good idea to cut off especially good specimens – the flowers of *Echinops exaltatus* can reach a diameter of 7cm (3in) – and dry them separately in silica gel, air drying the stems and foliage before glueing them back together. For smaller arrangements you may even want to mount them on florist's wires, although it would be a great pity to lose the interesting colour and texture of the thistle stems and it might be best to plan a tall arrangement to fit around them.

Erica cinerea

BELL HEATHER
Ericaceae

E. TETRALIX

E. VAGANS

E. cinerea is the genuine heather found wild in Britain – see the entry under *Calluna vulgaris* – and available as cullivay in a wide range of shades of rose, pink, purple, and the so-called lucky white. These can be grown either in the garden, or if you live in a suitable part of the world, the ordinary pink variety can be picked from the wild. There are many Ericas, including the wild species *Erica vagans* (CORNISH HEATH) and *Erica tetralix* (CROSS-LEAVED HEATH), which will grow in a temperate climate and may be worth drying if you have access to them from the wild. There are also a number of greenhouse species, including the showy "Cape Heaths" whose woody species have the reputation of being among the most temperamental of cultivated plants.

On the other hand the temperate species are quite easy, although they are rather fussy about soil, needing acid peaty conditions and disliking lime. They should be propagated by cutting and need shearing if they grow too long and straggly. Mulch them occasionally with leaves or peat moss and they will be happy. If you happen to live by the seaside or in an area of sunshine and natural poor soils they will be particularly suitable plants.

Drying these temperate heaths and heathers couldn't be easier. You simply hang up cut bunches in a stream of moving air and allow the moisture to evaporate from them. It's best to pick them before maturity.

Eryngium spp.

SEA HOLLIES
Umbelliferae

E. GIGANTEUM

E. MARITIMUM

E. BOURGATI

Eryngium maritimum – COMMON SEA HOLLY – is found on beaches throughout Britain. It's a bluish, spiny, stiff plant whose leaves do look like an enlarged version of holly and it grows to about 60cm (2ft) high, with bluish flower heads 2.5cm (1in) or so in diameter.

Eryngium giganteum – GIANT SEA HOLLY, as its name suggests, is a more robust species. It hails from the Caucasus and reaches a height of 1.2m (4ft) with flowers up to 10cm (4in) long and much larger leaves and bracts. There are a number of other cultivated sea hollies of which *Eryngium bourgati* and *Eryngium amethystinum* with its bright blue flowers might be suitable for drying.

These plants all like well-drained sandy soil, and will even thrive when gravel, broken stones and pieces of brick or old turves have been dug into a border. They like sun and shouldn't be moved once they have become established, although you may have to do so if you wish to split them by division. They can also be raised from seed sown in mid-spring – the seeds like sand too – or from root cuttings grown in free draining compost during the autumn.

Although the flowers can be dried in a moving airstream, the leaves, particularly those of *Eryngium maritmum* can be rather fleshy and could need quite warm air to dry them properly. If so, make sure that you pick the flowers early, before they have reached full maturity. Alternatively, you could try preserving the whole plant systematically with glycerine or glycol (see instructions under "Preserving with Glycerine") in order to try and obtain more natural and flexible foliage.

Gomphrena globosa — GLOBE AMARANTH
Amaranthaceae

Gypsophila paniculata — GYPSOPHILA
Caryophyllaceae

G. PANICULATA 'BRISTOL FAIRY'

At first sight this plant looks like a giant variety of clover except for leaves that are wider towards the stalk and bluntly pointed rather than the familiar clover trefoil. The flowers come in a variety of colours, yellow, orange, pink, purple or off-white with two bracts at the base. They are excellent for bedding or drying and the plant is usually grown as a half-hardy annual. The seeds need to germinate in a warm greenhouse in mid-spring and harden off for a week or two in a cold frame before being planted out in the garden. Alternatively, they can be transplanted into successively larger pots and kept warm in order to provide more showy specimens. For flower drying it might be worth trying both methods, the second in order to provide better quality blooms for display, the first to provide masses of varied background colour. The plants that are kept under glass should have rich soil with liquid manure applied to it at least once a week during the growing season. Indoors and outdoors they like plenty of light – this means a sunny bed in the garden.

The Globe Amaranth is well known as an "everlasting" plant and can be easily dried. For this the stems should be cut before the flowers reach maturity, tied loosely in not too large bunches – remember there may be several flowers on each branching stem – and hung in a current of warm moving air.

This plant is known as Baby's Breath in the United States. This name describes to perfection the billowy masses of white flowers on forking flower stems which grace this well-known perennial throughout the early and mid-part of the summer.

There has been a total breakthrough in the plant world with the variety "Bristol Fairy" – again an extremely descriptive title – which has produced quantities of slightly larger mauve flowers and is widely grown by commercial growers on Guernsey. It mixes very well with cut flowers and its more interesting size and colour should make it attractive to the flower drier.

As perennial, Gypsophila can be propagated by cuttings, but also grows well from seed sown in light soil during early spring. It doesn't like being moved once it's established and loves a loose limy soil, such as one containing old mortar or masonry, hence its name *Gypsophila* – "liking gypsum", (a lime-bearing rock).

The flowers are easy to dry in a moving current of dry air, but do tend to shrivel slightly. It's not easy to see a way round this since there are so many blooms and the stems are too widespread for silica gel to be used. It might be worth trying a stem or two in glycerine to see whether it will provide a supple smoother finish to the flowers.

Helichrysum bracteatum

STRAWFLOWER
Compositae

This is another genus of the Daisy family which lacks the flat, strap-shaped ray florets of the Daisy and only has the central disc ones. What look like ray florets in Helichrysum are in fact bracts developed from leafy material. They are the most conspicuous parts of these "everlasting" flowers or "immortelles" – names also given to Helipterum, Anaphalis, Ammobium and Xeranthemum – and at first glance would appear to be petals.

The genus contains a large number of species but this is the most popular. It's an annual seen in large numbers in very many commercial dried flower arrangements, but it's no worse for that. It's easy to grow in well-drained soils although it won't stand frost and likes sunshine. Its bracts are available in a variety of bright colours, yellow, orange, crimson or in plain white. Sow the seeds outside where you want them to flower and thin the plants to about 20cm (8in) apart. For earlier harvesting they can be sown under glass at about 16°C (60°F) and hardened off before planting out.

The heads are easy to dry by being hung in a current of warm moving air out of the light. They can fade badly and commercially some growers speed up this process by placing them in a water bath in a well ventilated area.

Caution: the heads are often cut off with very little stem and wired for use in arranging. if you want to do this you must insert florist's wire into the cut-off flowerhead while it is still fresh, otherwise it will be too hard. The sap acts as a kind of cement and holds the head in place on the wire after it has dried.

**Helipterum
manglesii**

HELIPTERUM
Compositae

H. ROSEUM

Extensive cross-naming occurs with this plant. That is to say, the same plant may be found under several different generic names: *Helipterum*, *Rhondanthe*, or *Acroclinum*. If you can't find the name *Helipterum* in your seedsman's catalogue, try looking for it under the other names.

Both the genera *Helipterum* and *Helichrysum* are named after the Greek god of the sun "Helios" but *Helichrysum* means "Sun Gold" – the original flowers being golden coloured; while *Helipterum* means "Sun Winged" or "Sun Feathered". I'm sure if you grow and dry either of these species you'll agree that the names are most appropriate. Even if their flowers are not by any means golden coloured the warmth and vitality which they'll bring into your homes in the depth of winter will make you think of blazing hot summer days.

Although there are a number of species of *Helipterum*, only the annual ones are worth growing without a greenhouse, and even with one the perennials are quite difficult. Sow the annuals in seed boxes in early spring and plant them out after the frosts have passed. They can be sown where they are to bloom but will flower rather late. *Helipterum manglesii* has pink, purple or white bracts, *Helipterum roseum* bright pink ones, and *Helipterum humboldtianum* has yellow flowerheads but much more lightly packed together in clusters.

All three can be dried in warm moving air.

Hydrangea spp. HYDRANGEA
Saxifragaceae

Lagenaria siceraria BOTTLE GOURD
Cucurbitaceae

There are numbers of different species and varieties of this showy, hardy or half-hardy shrub, which can be grown under glass or in the garden, although there they do need a considerable amount of space if they are to make the impressive display of which they are capable.

They come in all sorts of different colours and sizes, like acid soil, and should be propagated by cuttings. For more detailed growing instructions you are referred to specialists books on the subject.

Some people dry Hydrangeas by hanging the blooms head downwards in a moving current of warm air. This is a case, incidentally, where the blooms are large enough to be suspended individually by a piece of string tied with a clove-hitch around the woody stem. We feel that better quality is likely to be attained by using silica gel for drying. In this case, strip most of the leaves from the stem, and place it, flower head upwards, through either a piece of strong wire mesh covered in paper, or a polystyrene ceiling tile. Either of these supports should be built into a cardboard container, designed to fit around the individual flower head, and strong enough to support the weight of head and mesh. Then sprinkle silica gel carefully over, under, and around the head, taking care to get it in contact with all sides of the flowers, so that it both dries and supports them. Leave the flower to dry for several weeks, and carefully brush away the drying medium.

This is an annual climber with heart-shaped leaves and large white flowers that develop into gourds. It should be grown in a sheltered part of the garden and provided with support such as a trellis to climb up. This gives it the opportunity to grow rapidly and reach its maximum length of 4.5–6m (15–20ft).

The plants like rich soil – using plenty of rotted manure or compost – and should be grown from seed in a heated frame or greenhouse and planted out when all danger of frost is over. If you haven't space for so long a vine, pinch out the growing tip when it has reached 2 or 3m (8 or 10ft) and allow side shoots to develop.

It's a good idea to leave the gourds on the plant as long as possible. You can pull the vine from its supports, lay the grouds on plastic sheeting and cover them with cloches. Or you could grow the whole plant in a greenhouse and allow the gourds to ripen until the vine has dried and withered.

Then remove the gourds and allow them to dry in a warm place till they are light brown. Dip them in boiling water and wipe with a cloth to remove any skin. They can then be wax polished or hung up as they are. Some people like to leave the seeds in so that they can rattle them or even add handles to a couple of gourds and make a pair of primitive maracas. Traditionally the seeds were removed and the gourds were used as bowls or bottles. What I'd suggest is that you should paint vivid designs and patterns on them, then hang them up in a porch or over a fireplace and they will give you pleasure for several seasons. Brightly coloured acrylic paints such as those sold by artist's suppliers would be good for this. Don't wax the gourds first or the paint won't stick to them.

Lavandula spp.   LAVENDER
Labiatae

Leucadendron argenteum   SILVER TREE
Proteaceae

This is an aromatic plant and an important source of lavender oil for the perfume industry. Traditionally Lavender was used as a strewing plant to cover the floor and provide a pleasant scent when trampled. It is also one of the earliest air freshener. A small pile of the dried plant was burnt in a container and the smell of the essential oil plus the slightly acrid smell of burning effectively masked any unpleasant odours.

There seems to be some confusion about the nomenclature of the species, English Lavender grown in England for oil, being known as *Lavandula angus folia* or *Lavandula vera* and French Lavender being originally known as both *Lavandula officinalis* and *Lavandula vera*. The more broad-leaved Spike Lavender is known as *Lavandula spica*.

Lavender likes a sunny well-drained slope, if possible facing south and with not too rich a soil – a well-drained loam is probably most suitable. Over rich conditions encourage leaf formation, which is as undesirable for the flower dryer as it is for the commercial grower. The plant can be easily propagated by cuttings taken in late summer or early autumn and kept in a cold frame for planting out next spring. Commercially, the plants are grown in rows 60cm (2ft) apart with 45cm (18in) between the plants, but closer will do for the ordinary garden. Unlike the commercial grower, you will not be concentrating on the content of the oil or its quality, so pick your lavender when it has the best colour, erring on the side of immaturity. The flowers do tend to fade slightly. If you have too many flowers for decoration, you might try stripping some of them from their branches, putting them into a small bag of loosely woven material and tying it shut, perhaps with a pretty ribbon. These lavender bags can then be hidden among the sheets or underwear, a way of scenting them known to our mothers and grandmothers before them.

There's a certain amount of double nomenclature going on here, since *Leucadendron* means "silver", so we have literally "the silvery white tree". This is a very appropriate name for the downy, spear-shaped, tightly packed leaves of this South African native.

Like all the Proteaceae it is rather tricky to grow, even in a greenhouse, and is only for the most enthusiastic flower dryer. In the warmest part of Great Britain, namely the Scilly Isles, and in the Southern United States, it can be grown out of doors, but even there doesn't live very long. As a greenhouse species, it's perhaps best grown in a good-sized container so that it can be stood outside on warm summer days. It likes well-drained peaty soil and can be very tricky to nurse through its first few years, being susceptible to overwatering and the presence of lime. Seed will germinate in a warm greenhouse.

Most material of Leucadendron species is seen in flower arrangements imported in the dried state. Those of you who are lucky enough to have fresh material available might consider preserving some of it with glycerine in order to avoid its brown appearance.

If you're going to go to the trouble of growing the genus, you might as well grow a more showy species, such as *Leucodendron grandiflorum*. Be really ambitious and try drying it face upward in silica gel.

Liatris spicata
BLAZING STAR
Compositae

Limonium spp.
STATICE
Plumbaginaceae

L. SINUATIUM (DRIED)

L. SINUATIUM

This is a native of the eastern third of the United States. It's a hardy perennial with an upright spike of pink, purple or white flowers, opening from the top downward and providing showy material for drying or the border.

These plants like well-drained soil but at the same time grow better under quite rich conditions, so compost should be dug into the ground before they are planted. They also like a top dressing of compost or leaf mould. Other than this, do not disturb them. If these conditions are not available, it may be necessary to lift them like Dahlias and replant them next season. Propagate by dividing the roots in spring or by seed in a cold frame at this time of year. They may also be sown in early autumn and overwintered. Do not allow the mature plants to dry out – they should be watered and perhaps mulched in dry weather.

Because of the way in which the flowers ripen, some will be unopened towards the bottom of the spike while others are turning brown at the top of it. To avoid this pick the spikes before the flowers at the top have reached maturity and strip off the buds from the bottom before drying the spike. If you want to be very crafty you could take flowers of approximately the same maturity from several stems and wire them either onto one natural stem or a made-up one. If you do this it might be worth drying the individual florets in drying mixture, otherwise you can simply air dry the whole stem.

L. LATIFOLIUM

L. SUWOROWII

These plants are also known as "Sea Lavenders", although the common "Sea Lavender" – *Limonium vulgare*, found growing wild on British saltmarshes, is not as far as we know ever used for drying. The Winged Sea Lavender or Statice (its European equivalent), *Limonium sinuatium*, is one of the commonest commercially dried flowers. It is usually grown under plastic tunnels and sold in flower shops and garden centres. But it does not seem to be so well known as a species for home drying, perhaps because it is only hardy in the warmer regions, preferring a night temperature of some 10°C (50°F). Although it is a perennial in its native habitat in gardens it is usually grown as an annual and produces quantities of tough winged stems topped by abundant flowers whose calyxes may be purple or pink, pleated and persistent around smaller white or yellowish-white petals, or which may have predominantly wholly white or purple flowers. Other species are *Limonium latifolium* – a hardy perennial with mauve, pink or purplish flowers, *Limonium bonduelli* – similar to *Limonium sinuatium* but with yellow flowers, and *Limonium suworowii*, a large plant, with pinkish or lilac coloured flowers.

All species can be grown from seed, either sown where the plant is to flower or earlier in spring in a greenhouse. Both of the tenderer species (*Limonium bonduelli* and *L. latifolium*) benefit from greenhouse cultivation, especially in cooler areas. They like a light loam and can also be propagated by cuttings.

Statice is an easy plant to dry, its papery calyxes feel almost dry while they are still growing. Still, they need keeping away from strong light while they are being air dried or the colours can fade badly.

Lonas annua   AFRICAN DAISY
Compositae

Lunaria annua   HONESTY or MOONWORT
Cruciferae

LUNARIA SP.

Also known as *Lonas inodora*, this is an attractive plant native to the Mediterranean and belonging to the Daisy family but without the flat ray florets of the Daisy. Its slightly dome-shaped bright yellow flowers consist entirely of disc florets and form dense heads that last well in the garden and dry easily.

The plants like light well-drained soils and plenty of sunshine. They can be sown where they are to flower and thinned to about 15cm (6in) apart, or plants can be raised in a warm greenhouse and hardened off before being planted out when all danger of frost has passed.

The flowers can be dried in a moving current of warm dry air and should be cut when they are fully open but before any deterioration or fading.

A more descriptive Latin name would be the old one for this plant, *Lunaria biennis* for it is, in fact, a biennial requiring two years to make its best growth, although it has been grown as an annual. It's an old cottage garden plant with pink or purple scented flowers and elliptical white seedpods. These provide the genus with its Latin name *Lunaria* because their white sheen resembles that of the moon. No-one seems to know the origin of the English name perhaps it comes from the fact that the dried pods are transparent enough to be easily seen through.

To grow the plant as a biennial, sow the seed in late spring and plant out the young plants in early autumn. They like quite a light soil and semi-shade and once established will probably self-seed freely. There is also a PERENNIAL HONESTY (*Lunaria rediva*) which can be propagated by division.

The white central wall of the seedpod is the part used as a dried decoration. For this the outside parts should be stripped off carefully. Some people like to pick the seed heads as soon as the green colour has left them, maintaining that further exposure to the weather will discolour them. The heads are then dried in a moving air current. Others leave the pods on the plants until they are completely dry or even allow the weather to skeletonize them. In either case they must be handled carefully because they are very fragile. Dyeing is also a possibility and this is often done commercially. Obviously with such thoroughly dead material you have no option but to use the "dunk it" method. (See the section on glycerine preservation and drying.)

Molucella laevis   BELLS OF IRELAND
Labiatae

Nicandra physaloides   SHOO-FLY PLANT
Solanaceae

This plant is a native of the Middle East and closely related to the Dead Nettle, though at first glance this doesn't seem likely. The erect stems have closely packed flowers whose prominent part is a large green conical calyx with blunt points on its rim. Nestling in the bottom of this, the petals have the characteristic hooded, double-lipped structure of the Labiatae.

Molucella likes a fertile well-drained soil. Its seeds should be sown in a warm greenhouse and planted out after danger of frost is over. This will give it a good start. Allow about 30cm (12in) between plants and stake them if necessary.

This is a popular flower for commercial flower dryers but does require careful treatment.

The green calyxes turn white on drying and the best way to keep them in good condition is to plunge the freshly cut material *immediately* into a glycerine mixture. This should be prepared by adding one part of glycerine to two parts of hot water (very hot but not boiling). Stir, allow the mixture to cool and take it out into the garden. Cut the stems of *Molucella* diagonally with a sharp knife and at once place them in the mixture. When you have as many stems as can conveniently be placed in the container, take it back into the house and allow the glycerine mixture to rise slowly up the plants until it reaches the flowers. Then remove the plants from the mixture, wipe off any drops of glycerine which may have been exuded from them, and hang them up to dry.

This plant is a native of South America and is sometimes called "Apple-of-Peru". Its other English name refers to the fact that it has been used to drive away insects.

It is an annual growing up to about 1.2m (4ft) high, whose blue flowers have a winged calyx. In this are found the seeds and the whole fruit formed by it is the part of interest to flower dryers.

Like most half-hardy to hardy annuals *Nicandra* can be grown either from seed where it is to flower or can be given a better start by being raised in a greenhouse. In this case the seeds should be sown under warm conditions and hardened off under glass before being planted out in late spring. The plants like a well-drained rich soil with plenty of moisture and sun, although they will grow under ordinary garden conditions. It might be worth growing them with their roots in the shade and their heads in sunshine.

When the flowers are over and the fruits well-formed, long stems should be cut and hung in a current of moving warm air until the fruits are dry. They look good placed among foliage – this is the reason for cutting them with long stems, it's always easier to shorten than lengthen – and used as a basis for other arrangements.

Nigella damascena   LOVE-IN-A-MIST
Ranunculaceae

Papaver spp.   POPPY
Papaveraceae

This is an elegant plant with finely divided leaves, and solitary white or blue flowers. These will make a pretty display in the garden. Some can be cut, but for our purposes allow a fair number to develop into seedpods because these are the parts that are desirable for "flower" drying.

The plants are quite hardy but the seedlings don't like being moved, so seed should be scattered in the border where you want them to flower and the young plants thinned to a spacing of about 20cm (8in). You can also regiment the plant by planting it in straight lines, but perhaps this relaxed gypsy of a flower should be allowed better things than this.

The pods are easy to dry by being cut when they are well swollen, tied in loose bunches and hung in a warm current of moving air. If you feel daring you could try cutting one or two of the blooms with short stems and drying them face upwards in silica gel, using a support of polystryrene or cardboard, with holes cut in it. Take care to brush the powder carefully among the delicate styles and stamens and remember that when dried they will be even more fragile.

The seed heads are the parts used by arrangers and these imported in large quantities, mostly from the Mediterranean and Middle East. The home arranger will probably either have to spend money on splendid imported specimens or be content with the smaller examples that he has grown in his own garden. I have even seen seed heads of the once-common Corn Poppy (*Papaver rhoeas*) used in flower arrangements, although you will have to be diligent to find specimens of this nowadays because of the widespread use of modern herbicides.

Even the opium poppy (*Papaver somniferum*), named for the

36

Physalis alkekengi CHINESE LANTERN
Solanaceae

P. RHOEAS

drowsiness produced by its extracts, has been used for arranging on occasions. Although it cannot legally be cultivated without a licence, it is still found growing in cottage gardens or in the wild and the seeds, which contain no drug, are used for decorating bread and cakes.

Poppies thrive in most garden soils. They like full sun and the seeds may be sown in spring where the plants will flower.

In a good year all these seeds can be allowed to dry out on the plant, or you can pick them and hang them up in a loose bunch in gently moving air. Even the normal stipulation about avoiding sunlight is not quite so important in this case.

In this plant the fruits are surrounded by a swollen coral red to orange "lantern", pointed at the bottom, flat on top, 5–7.5cm (2–3in) long and somewhat resembling the lightshades that are sold by Chinese emporia. These are the parts that give the plant its English names "Chinese Lantern" for variety *franchetii*. "*Bladder Cherry*" is the ordinary variety, the generic name is derived from the Greek *phusa*, meaning a bladder. Both these closely related hardy perenials are also known as "Winter Cherry".

The fruits of both the ordinary variety and its relative the Cape Gooseberry, (*P. peruviana*) are often eaten, although the latter needs greenhouse cultivation. They should all be allowed to ripen fully before they are tasted, otherwise they may contain traces of poisons.

Both species grow well in ordinary garden soil. Propagation is by division in autumn or winter and new stock can also be raised from seed.

For the arranger they make an attractive decoration which should be picked before rain has damaged them. They can then be allowed to dry in a cool place, perhaps stood upright in a vase to prevent damage and with a current of air blowing round them.

ROSES
Rosaceae

ROSA SP.

ROSA SP.

This is one of the best loved and most widely grown of all garden plants. There are many varieties giving a vast range of shape and colour to choose from.

Roses for drying are more successful if they are specially cultivated for they should have long stiff stems and flowers which, although of good form, are not so full of petals that their density prevents the drying process. Varieties commonly used are "Columbia", "Ophelia", "Madame Butterfly", "Richmond" and "Roselandia".

Some roses are grown under glass for cut flowers and preservation, and usually climbing versions of hybrid tea roses are selected for this type of husbandry. Roses grow well in heavy soil in a variety of situations. They dislike being dry at the roots and, since they have a shallow root system, they must be watered in dry weather. Hoeing or forking of roses in their root zone should be avoided since this causes much damage to their root systems. Instead regular mulches of manure or other humus-forming material should be applied around the stems of the plants each autumn. Regular insecticidal sprays to keep down insect pests and fungicidal sprays to combat mildew and black spot are needed. Roses are normally propagated by budding when named varieties are grafted onto briar rootstocks using the "budding" method of achieving such a union.

Unfortunately, they are not the easiest plants to dry. Although it has been traditional to dry bridal bouquets containing roses by hanging them up in warm air – perhaps in the airing cupboard – this has not generally produced good results. The flowers, even in the bud stage, tend to look forlorn and provide a beautiful memento of a sentimental occasion only for those who actually took part in it. The airing cupboard is not a place we would recommend for drying any flowers.

Big commercial growers do dry their roses in warm moving air. For them this is presumably a matter of compromise with the speedy cheap nature of the process and general willingness to accept a certain lack of quality. They also use small-flowered varieties and often buds. For the do-it-yourself enthusiast there is really only one answer – silica gel. With this medium sometimes even the larger more delicate varieties can be dried, but it is still difficult, and a great deal of care and perseverance is essential. The petals must be coated evenly, making sure that they are supported by the powder. Use fine powder and remove it carefully. Brush away any remaining traces with the greatest of care and don't expect success on every occasion.

Ruscus aculeatus   BUTCHER'S BROOM
Liliaceae

ROSA SP. (DRIED)

ROSA SP. (DRIED)

Botanically this is a strange plant, a shrub with spiny flattened branches that look like leaves and that bear the flowers. The real leaves are small brown scales about 6mm ($\frac{1}{4}$in) long. The female and male plants are separate, and it's possible to end up with a garden filled with one or the other, because the plant is usually propagated by division of the fleshy rootstocks or by taking suckers rather by seed, although hermaphrodites (both sexes on the same bush) are available.

It's possible to find this plant growing wild, but better foliage will generally be available from cultivated specimens all of which do well on ordinary garden soil and in dappled shade. It is also possible to eat the young shoots, although they look exceedingly unappetizing.

There are a number of other cultivated species of which *Ruscus hypoglossum* (LARGE BUTCHER'S BROOM) grows well in shady situations. *Ruscus aculeatus* thrives better on the edge of woodland, or among other bushes. These are its natural habitats.

This plant is a popular subject for dyeing, and because it is a tough specimen, timber dyes might be the cheapest alternatives. Failing this, try florist's dyes. Follow them all by a glycerine and water mixture, made up in two parts to one glycerine to water, using very hot but not boiling water and allowing it to cool before immersing the stems. These should be cut diagonally with a sharp knife shortly before they are put in the mixture. Use a soft cloth to wipe off any beads of glycerine, which after a while may appear on the leaves. When they have fully darkened, remove the stems from the mixture and wipe the leaves and stem ends again.

Salvia spp.
SAGE
Labiatae

S. SPLENDENS

A number of different sages are found wild and in the garden. Indeed it's been suggested that the ordinary kitchen variety *Salvia officinalis* dried properly, could give a delicate aroma to flower arrangements. We tend to think that the most suitable place for this is in the centre of a roasted chicken or turkey. There are traditionally a multitude or practical and medicinal uses for the Common Sage – hence the name of the genus, from the Latin *Savus* – "*Safe*", but this seems the one which is most worth preserving.

However, there are some magnificent ornamental species, including *Salvia farinacea* with purplish-blue flowers, which grows up to 91cm (3ft) tall. *Salvia splendens* (SCARLET SAGE) is a shrubby plant up to the same size with vivid red flowers, and *Salvia patens* (BLUE SAGE) has blue or white flowers, but is a bit shorter. All these should be grown as half-hardy annuals.

Salvia patens is usually raised from seed which has to be sown in heat early in the year to give seedlings a good start. These need to be well hardened off before planting outside when all danger of frost is passed. Alternatively, they may be grown in containers, or beds in a greenhouse, or under polythene. Light, well ventilated conditions are needed for protected crops. *Salvia farinacea* also is best treated as an annual. Cultivation is as described for *Salvia patens* except that it requires plenty of room to develop its high flowering spikes.

Sages can be easily dried in warm moving air although this does tend to make the foliage rather brittle. It's not easy to see how to overcome this, although it might be possible, but prohibitively expensive, to dry the whole plant in a flat box of silica gel. Perhaps in *Salvia patens* and *Salvia farinacea* the larger lower leaves could be stripped off before drying in gel, but this hardly seems possible for the other species.

Solidago spp.
GOLDENRODS
Compositae

Solidago comes from the Latin, meaning "to make whole", "to heal". In the old days, it was used as a herbal remedy for bleeding, although Gerard in his *Herbal* comments that people were only willing to pay good money for it while it was considered to be a rare plant. As soon as it was found growing wild near London, herbalists went looking for other rarer species.

There is a native British species, *Solidago vigaurea* probably not worth drying if you have access to the cultivated ones. These are native to North America, where the genus is a widespread wild plant. *Solidago canadensis* was the original import, but both this plant and its relatives have been bred for cultivation and a number of different varieties such as "Golden Wings", and a number of dwarf ones, are available.

Goldenrods may be raised from seed, but normal propagation is by division in either autumn or spring. The plants thrive in poor soil and in rough areas amongst rocks.

Goldenrod is an easy plant to dry, and can just about be dried on the plant, although better quality will be obtained by picking it and drying it in bunches in a current of warm, moving, dry air.

Typha latifolia/
Typha angustifolia

REEDMACES
Typhaceae

These plants are commonly known as "Bullrushes" but that name should be given to the Sedge *Scirpus lacustris*, which has a much more grassy-looking appearance than these robust plants, with their cylindrical brown flower spikes of female flowers, topped by a smaller spike of yellow male ones. The difference between the two species is mainly one of size.

These aquatic natives of Europe and Asia are hardy plants which normally grow in marshes, as marginal water plants and which each grow up to 60cm (2ft) deep in water. The roots are thick and fleshy and they may be divided in spring to increase stock. Typha spreads naturally because its seed when fully ripe is carried long distances in the wind – the seed having silky appendages rather like a dandelion. The plants are not particular about soil conditions and thrive equally well in clay marshes and peat bogs.

These rushes continue to ripen, for instance, if they're left in their natural habitat at the edge of a pond, until the seeds are ready to be distributed during the warm weather of the following year. They look beautiful with their rich brown colours against the winter snow, but if you bring them into a warm room they will ripen much more quickly because the room's warmth behaves as a substitute for the following spring weather. The result is that you are likely to come down one winter morning, and find a corner of your room full of bullrush seeds. They are quite soft and fluffy and if a slight breeze or a draught has been blowing across the room, they will have wafted into every little nook and cranny and be stuck firmly into the fibres of your carpets. Different people have different solutions to this problem, the commonest being to spray the heads with hair lacquer. But as David Carter comments, "Bullrushes always win in the long run"!

If you still feel like drying them after this warning, it's not difficult. Simply stand them in a vase in the corner, as people have been doing for years. But be prepared to reach for the dustpan.

Verticordia spp.
JUNIPER MYRTLES
Myrtaceae

Xeranthemum annuum
EVERLASTING FLOWER
Compositae

This name literally means "heart turners", and although these evergreen shrubs are not "heart stoppers" they are quite readily cultivated, and dried too. They grow 61–122cm (2–4ft) high with hairy leaves and flat heads of flowers that have hairy petals. They must be grown under glass, but in the summer can be lifted out in their pots or containers to enjoy the sun.

Verticordia densiflora has very narrow leaves and pink or white flowers in clusters, 5–10cm (2–4in) in diameter. *Verticordia nitens* has orange to yellow flowers, and somewhat wider leaves. Both species are natives of Western Australia.

Dry the Juniper Myrtles by hanging them head downwards in loose cut bunches, in a warm moving airstream.

The Latin name of this plant means literally "Annual dried flower", while both the other names reflect the fact that it lasts for a long time, so it ought to be a favourite with flower dryers.

Xeranthemum is a member of the Daisy family, with central disc florets and long dry papery bracts in place of the Daisy's flat, strap-shaped ray florets. Its flowers are found in single and double varieties, and may be white, pink or purple.

The plants may be grown as hardy or half-hardy annuals, seed being sown either in the spring where the plants are to flower, or earlier, in the greenhouse, at a temperature of about 10°C (50°F). They are then pricked out before being hardened off under glass, and planted out in late spring or early summer. The directly sown plants merely need thinning to 15–23cm (6–9in) apart. As they grow to a height of about 61cm (2ft), they may need staking. Light, rather poor soil will encourage them to bloom freely.

They are easy plants to dry, being cut slightly before maturity, with long stems to aid in arranging, tied in loose bunches so that air can easily pass around them, and hung head downwards in a current of dry moving air. It's also possible to cut the heads off short, and use them for surface arrangements, on card, or for flat squat arrangements. This can be done with secateurs after the heads have dried on long stems, but if it is necessary to wire them in order to fasten them into the arrangement, this may be more easily done if the heads are cut while the stems are still fresh, and the wires inserted then.

THE GRASSES
Gramineae

The Grasses are an extremely important group of plants both economically and for flower dryers. They are also interesting botanically, being structurally quite unlike other flowering plant families.

Essentially they consist of a jointed stem, which is hollow between the joints and solid elsewhere. A tubular leaf sheath surrounds this and grows away from it, usually into a long thinnish, flattish leafy blade, although some grass leaves are U-shaped in cross-section, oval, or quite wide in proportion to their length.

Their stems may grow in tight clumps, which sometimes become dense. This usually happens in perennial grasses – those that live for a number of seasons. They may be solitary and upright, or prostrate, lying along the surface of the soil, or they may change their direction of growth, upright and prostrate stems being found within the same species. If their stems are prostrate, they may well root from the nodes, and send up fresh leaves and flowering stems. Prostrate stems growing on the surface are known as "stolons" and, as its name suggests, are found in CREEPING BENT (*Agrostis stolonifera*) a common grass that grows as a weed in pastures, and is also used for more specialized kinds of turf, such as putting greens or sports fields. If stems grow beneath the surface they are known as rhizomes. Every gardener will be familiar with *Agropyron repens*, "COUCH" or "TWITCH GRASS", whose creeping rhizomes allow it to spread throughout the garden, always seeming to come from beyond the neighbour's fence, and resisting so many attempts to eradicate it. Its rhizomes break in the gardener's hands and the pieces then develop into new plants, so the struggle to get rid of it begins again.

Where the leaf blades join the sheaths, the grasses develop a characteristic ring of tissue, known as "ligule". Often this is thin and membranous, sometimes it is hairy, or it may be missing. I remember as an agriculture student being taught a little verse, in order to distinguish the immature plants of three common species of cereals. This mnemonic referred to the ligule, and was used when the leaf blade was pulled gently so that the sheath came away from the stems and the ligule was visible.

> "*Barley big and bare,*
> *Wheat wee and woolly,*
> *Oats none at all*".

One of the fascinating parts of grass structure is the flower. This is complicated, and often very small, needing a hand lens or even a low-powered microscope, if it is to be clearly seen. Only a brief outline of its structure is given here. For a more detailed description consult any specialist book, such as C.E. Hubbard's *Grasses*.

What we usually think of as the grass "flower" is, in fact, a number of spikelets. Sometimes these are borne individually on thin stalks, branching out on either side of a main stem. Other species

have spikelets that grow directly on the main stem, in a more or less continuous spike.

On the outside of each spikelet there are usually two bracts called "glumes", which surround the rest of the flower at least until it opens. The flower generally consists of two other bracts, the "lemma" and "palea", containing the sexual parts – ovary, stigma, and anthers. There are often a number of flowers within the glumes, sometimes as many as 20, each enclosed in a lemma and palea. In other species there is only one flower per spikelet.

For the sake of simplicity throughout this book we have referred to a collection of spikelets as a flower "spike" or "flowerhead", ignoring the fact they they can be organized into other more technical classifications, based upon the exact way in which the spikelets are arranged. Anyone wishing to understand those in more detail should consult a specialist book.

From the point of view of flower dryers, these flower spikes and spikelets are the most important parts of the grass. Often the spikes have attractive shapes, influenced by the appearance of the spikelets, and the way in which they are arranged. Sometimes the spikelets have bristles or "awns" sticking out from them, attached to the glumes or the inner parts of the grass flowers. The spikelets are the parts for which, in a sense, we are drying the grasses, because while the leaves in some species may be attractive, in others they shrivel and twist in drying, and end up looking quite uninteresting.

A point of some importance about all this is that spikelets of grass flowers have a tendency, especially marked in certain species, to "shed" or "shatter" when they are being dried. This means that either the whole spikelet or the individual florets within it drop out, leaving only the glumes. Sometimes the spikelets break up and some or all of their parts fall out. The exact technical terminology does not really matter. What does matter is that the unfortunate flower dryer is left with a messy or boring looking inflorescence instead of the shapely flowerhead that they picked from their garden.

Where individual species are known to be liable to shedding or shattering, a warning has been included in the drying instructions. However, we must emphasize that care should be taken when drying almost all grasses – a notable exception is perhaps a grass such as Maize, whose flower structure is completely different. This warning applies especially to those that are to be dyed, since the extra amount of drying involved is particularly likely to cause problems. We have also recommended the use of warm air only in those cases where the grass flowerhead is unusually massive. Here the extra moisture which it contains may need such treatment. Otherwise, we believe that warm air may very well increase the chances of shattering without necessarily improving the quality of the dried grass. Warm air drying may be used if speed is important, but generally this is not so, at least for amateur dryers.

Agrostis elegans   SLENDER BENT GRASS

Agrostis nebulosa   CLOUD BENT GRASS

A. PULCHELLA

This is a tufted grass with narrow leaves, a native of the Western Mediterranean. It grows to about 30cm (1ft) tall and has tiny spikelets on short stalks and a branching flowerhead. Our illustration shows a similar species which has been lightly dyed to enhance its colour.

Sow seed in spring where the plants are to flower in good garden soil, or treat as a biennial by sowing in early autumn and allowing them to overwinter. This will give more robust plants.

Cut the stems before the flowers are fully ripe, otherwise you may have trouble with shedding of the flower parts. Tie a bundle of grasses tight enough to prevent their stems falling out, but with the stems slightly across each other, so that the flowerheads are somewhat separate. Hang this bundle head downwards in a dark place and in a current of moving air. The heads and stems can be dyed by immersion in a bath of dye (the "dunkit" method), and should then be re-dried carefully to prevent shattering.

This is a tufted annual from Spain that can grow up to 37cm (15in) high and has small spikelets on short stalks in a branching flowerhead.

Sow seeds where you want the plant to flower in ordinary to good garden soil. This should be done in spring. Alternatively, in autumn or late summer sow seed so that the plant overwinters and produces strong growth for the next season.

Use a sharp pair of scissors to gather the flower stems before the heads are fully ripe – this helps to prevent damage from shattering of the spikelets. Tie the stems together so that the heads flop apart slightly and so are in a position to receive free air flow. Then dry them in the dark, in a moving air current. After this they can be dyed and dried again, even more care being taken to avoid accidental damage.

Aira elegantissima   HAIR GRASS

Avena sterilis   ANIMATED OAT

Also known as *Aira elegans* or *Aira capillaris*, Hair Grass is a slender annual grass from the Mediterranean region, which grows from 15–45cm (6–18in) tall, and has an open branching, flowerhead with small silvery spikelets and very fine branches. Its leaves are like hairs, hence its English name.

This elegant grass should be sown in a normal to light soil in early spring, and allowed to grow where it is to flower. It likes a certain amount of shade.

Cut the flower stems, pick some leaves to go with them and, tying them all in a loose bundle, hang this where there is a moving current of air.

This is a grass from the Mediterranean region and a close relative of the important agricultural crop Oats (*Avena sativa*), as well as of the Wild Oat (*Avena fatua*) – the False Oat – (literally "Silly Oat") which closely mimics this, and for a long time was an awkward weed in grain crops because it was difficult to remove with selective herbicides. Sometimes it also mimics the Animated Oat, although that has longer spikelets and arms. In *Avena sterilis* these are particularly prominent and twist and untwist with variation in the humidity of the atmosphere. It may be that this is a mechanism which helps the seeds to be drawn into the soil so that it can germinate.

Avena sterilis can grow up to 1.2m (4ft) tall, and has loose flowerheads, like the oat, with spikelets up to 4cm (1½in) long. It likes a sunny position and doesn't need anything special in the way of soil. Sow seed in spring where you want the grass to flower. Alternatively, treat it as a biennial and sow in early autumn so that it will overwinter and make better growth during the next growing season.

If any of you have access to the cultivated oat (*Avena sativa*) you might like to try growing this, but please take stray plants from field edges, not from the crop itself. *Avena fatua* can also be dried – it is usually found as a weed in other grain crops, and in this case you will be doing the farmer a favour. All three are good for dyeing by the "dunkit" method, after they have been dried (by being tied in bunches) in a stream of moving air.

This is a very attractive tufted annual grass native to the Mediterranean and growing up to 0.6m (2ft) high with sparse purplish coloured spikelets, up to 3cm (1in) long. These hang down and nod and tremble in the wind. A variety (*Briza maxima rubra*) is available that has bright red spikelets edged with white.

Seed should be sown either in spring or autumn in any fertile, well-drained, loamy garden soil, and in the place where the grass is to grow. It likes plenty of sunshine.

Drying is extremely easy. Simply cut the stems before the heads have reached maturity, and stand them in a container in a current of warm moving air. To make the most of the colour, the plant should be kept in the dark, and does not need to be hung head downwards, since this would tend to damage the stems of the drooping spikelets.

This grass grows wild throughout much of Europe, and for those of our readers who live in Britain, may provide an opportunity to dry a Quaking Grass without having to grow it in their gardens. It reaches about the same height as the other two species but its spikelets are intermediate, being somewhat larger than those of *Briza minor*, up to half the size of those found on *Briza maxima*, and purplish green in colour. It would, of course, be possible to grow a clump of this perennial grass in your garden. If you wish to do so, please leave the original clump unharmed and start the grass from seed. Sow in the spring where you'd like it to flower. As the plant is a perennial you won't have to repeat this process every year, which gives it a distinct advantage over the other *Briza* species.

To dry *Briza media* cut its flower stems and hang them head down in bunches to dry, in a current of moving air.

Briza minor SMALL QUAKING GRASS

Bromus briziformis

This is a tufted annual grass, generally about 30cm (1ft) high, although sometimes growing much larger. It has greenish nodding spikelets, about 0.5cm ($\frac{1}{4}$in) long and arranged in a loose branching flower head.

This plant should be grown from seed and sown in spring or autumn, where it is to flower. It likes fertile, well-drained garden soil, and plenty of sun.

To dry, cut the stems before they are fully mature, tie in bunches, and hang head downwards in a current of moving air. A dark place will give the best results.

This tufted annual or biennial grass grows up to about 60cm (2ft) high and is a native of Europe and Asia. Its flowerheads have drooping branches, with hanging spikelets about 2cm ($\frac{3}{4}$in) long. The leaves are hairy and taper to a fine point.

It's not at all fussy about soil and like other plants are annual or biennial can be sown either in spring or autumn. The latter practice allows growth before winter so that the plants have a good start in the next spring. They will grow in somewhat shaded or sunny conditions.

It's important to pick the flower spikes early if you want to dry them, otherwise there is considerable danger of shattering. Hang them head downwards in a cool, airy place and allow them to dry slowly. They can then be dyed by the "dunkit" method, but take care not to damage the spikelets, especially when you are redrying them.

Bromus madritensis   COMPACT BROME

Coix lacryma/Jobi   JOB'S TEARS

This European species contrasts strongly with *Bromus briziformis,* having a compact bristly flowerhead rather like an irregular brush. It's given this appearance by awns up to 2cm (¾in) long, emerging from the spikelets. The whole head is quite impressive, being capable of growing up to 12–15cm (5–6in) long.

Bromus madritensis is an annual or biennial quite often tufted which grows up to 60cm (2ft) tall. Although it grows in the wild in Britain, it can be cultivated. It needs ordinary garden soil and sun or semi-shade and should be sown in spring or autumn where it is to flower.

Dry the flowers by cutting the stems before the heads are too well developed, tying them loosely in bunches and allowing them to dry gently in a moving current of air. Hopefully this will prevent damage to the awns and spikelets. When the grass is dry it is a good subject for dyeing by immersion in florists' or other commercial dyes. If you do this please be careful not to damage the arms and spikelets because the character of the grass does depend on these.

This is a sturdy grass growing up to some 1.5m (5ft) high with broad pointed leaves and noticeably jointed stems. At the end of the stems are found swellings, which form the base of the spikelets and ripen into the plants fruits or "beads", becoming white, grey or purple. They have been used as food and medicine in the Far East and are often used as beads for children's toys.

The plant is best grown as a half-hardy annual, though it can be planted outdoors in late spring if you live in a warm area. Otherwise sow under glass with some heat in early spring to give it a good start, harden off gradually and plant out about 30cm (1ft) apart in reasonable garden soil and a sunny place. *Coix* does not like to become too dry, and should be watered in dry weather.

Cut the flowers with plenty of stem to give maximum scope for arranging, tie them up in bunches, and allow them to dry in moving air, in a dark place. The seeds can be stripped from the plants when they have dried, have holes bored in them, and then they can be used as beads. Alternatively, they can be picked from the plant while it's still in the ground, and dried separately.

Cortaderia selloana PAMPAS GRASS

Elymus arenarius LYME GRASS

This is an exceedingly robust perennial grass – a botanical way of saying that it grows very big, doesn't need resowing every year, and is useless for your garden, unless you have a large showy site for it. Its clumps of leaves can be 90–120cm (3–4ft) tall and often look a bit dried-up. They have sharp edges, so be careful! The flower spikes, which are long and plumed and very showy, can grow up to 3m (10ft) from the ground and be 90cm (3ft) long. I remember we used to tease and tickle each other with them when we were children. Usually the male and female spikes are on separate plants, and as is often the case, the females are more showy.

The plant likes a good supply of compost or manure, and deep cultivation before it is planted. Remember that it may remain in the same place for many years, and you should dig in plenty of manure or compost under it. Clip off any dead leaves, apply fertilizer once a year, and water the clumps if they become dry. It can be grown from seed or by division.

Cut the heads with good long stems, rather before they reach maturity and dry them by standing them upright in containers. Moving air is still necessary and although some authorities do recommend direct sunlight, we feel that this may contribute to the shedding of the decorative female flower plumes, something which can be a problem with this species. Pampas is a natural subject for dyeing, which can sometimes be taken to garish extremes. For a change try more subtle colours. Use the "dunkit" method and take care not to damage the flowerheads, especially when you are redrying them.

This is a sand-loving grass which grows near the sea-shore and is often planted to help keep sand-dunes in place. It's a stout, blue-green to grey perennial, which grows in tufts from long rhizomes, and can be too strong growing and invasive when planted in a garden. It has numerous spikelets, without bristles arranged in a cylindrical flowerheads, that may be over 30cm (1ft) in length.

If you're lucky enough to live near the seaside, in a sandy area with beach or dunes, you may be able to find this flower growing wild. If so, this is probably the best way to acquire it for drying. If not, it is perfectly possible to grow it in your garden. It will grow in ordinary soil, although as you might expect from its native habitat, it does prefer pure sand. There is a similar cultivated species *Elymus racemosus*, a native of Eastern Europe, which has more interesting shaped flowerheads that taper for at least their top third, and are pointed at the ends.

Propagate both species by division – the rhizomes grow easily – or if you have to, buy seed. The flower stems and leaves should be cut before the flowers are fully ripe and hung head downwards in bunches to dry.

Festuca ovina glauca   BLUE FESCUE

Hordeum jubatum   SQUIRREL TAIL GRASS

Also known as *Festuca glauca*, this is a variety of the common grass "Sheeps Fescue" which is widespread on moorlands, but unlike the wild species, this one is sufficiently interesting to be worth growing in the garden. Its tufted wiry leaves and upright irregular one-sided flower spikes are an attractive greenish blue, and make a pleasant edging to a flower border – the grass grows up to about 30cm (1ft) high – as well as being useful for drying.

This plant likes light sandy soil and can stand full sunshine. Propagate it by dividing existing clumps, because the seed is difficult to obtain from nurserymen.

Drying could not be easier. Hang bunches of the grass in a current of moving air. To keep strong leafy growth, it may be necessary to clip the leaves and old flower stems occasionally.

Also known as Fox Tail Barley, this is a North American weed whose long silvery green arms can be a serious nuisance to animals. This raises an interesting question as to when a weed is not a weed, since, for a flower dryer, they are highly decorative. Perhaps the best definition, and one that would be of use to all gardeners, says that "a weed is a plant growing where it isn't wanted!" This includes plants such as old potato tubers, growing on through next year's plot of cabbage.

Hordeum jubatum grows to about 75cm (2½ft) high, and although it is a perennial or biennial it is usually grown as an annual. It likes sun and apart from that any garden soil will suit it. The seed should be sown where the plant is to develop.

Drying is easy. Cut the flower stems well before the heads are fully mature and tie them up in bunches. Allow these to dry in a well ventilated dark place. Do not pick these too early, or dry them too fast, or you will encourage shattering.

Hordeum vulgare — CULTIVATED BARLEY

This is one of two species of Cultivated Barley, the other being *Hordeum distichon*. *Hordeum vulgare* has a four-sided spikelet and is the more common species in Europe.

It can be grown in ordinary garden soil, but is quite easy to gather from field corners, rather before harvest time. Please do not pick stems from the main field crop because this represents someone's livelihood, but confine yourself to the overshot and scattered plants that are always to be found on tracks and at field edges. But do not wait as late as harvest time before you pick your barley for drying. Farmers are aiming for a different state of dryness, which will allow the seeds to be readily separated during threshing. You, on the other hand, want the individual spikelets to remain on the flower spikes for as long as possible. On the other hand, it might be a good idea for you to pick one ripe head in order to thresh it yourself, and grow a small patch of barley in your garden next year.

Barley likes plenty of sunshine and is an easy plant to dry. Simply hang the plant downwards, in bunches, and allow a current of dry air to blow across it.

Lagurus ovatus — HARE'S TAIL

This is an attractive grass, up to 60cm (2ft) tall, whose oval flower spikes are thought to resemble a Hare's Tail, hence its name.

It likes the sun, well-drained garden soil, and is easily grown from seed, either as an annual or biennial. For the latter, sow it in pots in late summer or early autumn and keep it under glass for the winter. This gives it a distinct advantage in next spring's growth. As an annual it should be sown in spring where you want it to flower.

The flowering stems should be cut, tied in loose bundles, and hung head downwards in a warm airy place in the dark, until they have dried thoroughly. They can then, if you wish, be dried by immersion and re-dried carefully.

Miscanthus sinensis   EULALIA GRASS

M. SINENSIS 'ZEBRINUS'

Over a number of years, this grass will form a clump several feet across and at least 90cm (3ft) high. Its flowerheads are up to 37cm (15in) long and fan-shaped, curling over upon themselves. They are often reddish or purplish, and are formed in autumn. The grass has rough leaves, several feet long and up to 2.5cm (1in) wide. Variegated varieties are available – *Miscanthus sinensis variegatus* and *Miscanthus sinensis zebrinus* in which the variegated patches run crossways.

The plant likes sun and fertile soil, and may need to be cut back in springtime to get rid of dead leaves and encourage new growth. As it is a long-lived perennial species, occasional mulching or top dressing is an advantage.

Cut both flower stems and leaves with plenty of length, tie them in loose bunches and allow them to dry in a current of dry air.

M. SINENSIS VARIEGATUS

Oryza sativa   RICE

Panicum capillare   WITCH GRASS

P. VIRGATUM

This is one of the world's most important food crops and a somewhat demanding and exotic plant to grow for drying, so it is included chiefly for the enthusiast.

The seeds form the part that is eaten, sometimes in a polished white form. However, the unpolished "brown" rice contains more vitamins and protein.

It needs a temperature of about 21°C (70°F), so is a subject for a warm greenhouse. It should be grown in large pots, in fertile soil, and plenty of space should be left above the soil so that it can be covered in standing water. The seed should be planted in water under a layer of sand and the seedlings thinned to about 7.5cm (3in). When the plants are well established, the water level can be allowed to fall a little. The plants may well grow 1–1.5m (4–5ft) high, and have leaves up to 2.5cm (1in) wide.

For drying they should be harvested when the grains are swollen but before they have begun to ripen. Hang the cut flower stems in a current of warm moving air, and allow plenty of space around them. The variety *Oryza sativa nigrescens* with purple foliage would be an interesting one to grow, or possibly the wild variety *Oryza sativa rufipogon* which has long red bristles on its flower spikelets.

This is a tufted annual grass, native of North America and growing up to 76cm (2½ft) high. It has green or purplish flowers in large spreading flowerheads, and wavy margins to its leaves.

The plants like sunshine and are happy with ordinary garden soil. The seed should be sown in mid-spring where it is to grow.

Cut the flower stems and leaves before the flowers are fully ripe because they have a tendency to disintegrate on drying. Tie them in loose bunches and hang them head downwards in a moving airstream.

Panicum virgatum   SWITCH GRASS

This is a perennial grass from North America, which grows into a clump some 60cm (2ft) high, with quite narrow leaves, and large, loose, wide flowerheads.

It needs sunny conditions and reasonable garden soil and can be easily propagated by division. This should be repeated every few years, to make sure that the plants remain vigorous.

Another perennial, *Panicum obtusum*, the VINE MESQUITE, native of North America, can also be treated in this way. Both species can be dried easily by being cut before the flowerheads have ripened, tied in bunches, and hung head downwards in a moving current of air.

Panicum miliaceum   MILLET

This is a well-known food plant in China, Japan and India. Indeed, recently its grain has become quite well known in Europe and America, because of the wholefood movement.

It grows up to 90–120cm (3–4ft) tall with broad hairy leaves, and a flowerhead that, curling over to one side, has masses of densely packed small spikelets. It can be grown as an annual, in reasonable garden soil, being sown in spring where it is to flower.

To dry the flowers, cut the stems well before they're fully ripe and hang them in bunches in a warm dry current of air with plenty of space around the heads. Since they are not, in this case, being grown for food, it's important that they shouldn't have a chance to ripen, otherwise the spikelets could well become loose and be lost.

Pennisetum macrourum

This is a tufted perennial grass from South Africa that grows to a height of about 1.5m (5ft) and has flower spikes up to 30cm (1ft) long, with rough bristles.

It likes sun and a well-drained garden soil but will withstand frost. Propagate it by division in spring or early autumn.

The flowers dry easily but must be picked well before maturity in order to prevent damage to the spikelets. The stems should be cut and tied loosely in bunches, to allow air to reach the flowerheads easily. Then they should be hung head downwards in a current of cool moving air until dry. Do not dry the plant in direct sunlight because this will not help to prevent the spikelets shattering.

Pennisetum setaceum FOUNTAIN GRASS

Pennisetum villosum FEATHERTOP

Also known as *Pennisetum ruppelii*, this is a perennial grass from Africa and Asia that is often cultivated as an annual. It grows up to 90cm (3ft) high and forms a clump of narrow arched leaves topped by flower spikes up to 30cm (12in) long and with many slender bristles. These in turn are covered with feathery hairs.

This plant can be grown as an annual, being given either an early start as seed in a greenhouse, and planted out when it has developed, or in warmer parts being sown directly where it is to flower. As a perennial, it will only stand light frost and needs protection, or alternatively, should be lifted and stored in a cool place. The foliage can be clipped and the clumps divided into pieces suitable for starting off in small pots in the greenhouse.

Pick the flowers well before maturity. The stems should be tied in bunches and then hung head downwards in a moving current of cool air. Dyeing suits this species, but again you must be careful not to damage the spikelets. Use the "dunkit" method.

Pennisetum latifolium
This is a large perennial grass that can be grown outdoors in mild areas, or more successfully in a greenhouse. It has dense, wavy, drooping flowerheads, several inches long, and may reach 3m (10ft) in height.

If grown outside, freely drained soil, plenty of sun and shelter are needed. In cold winters it may be necessary to cover the plants against frost. Early in spring, clip back the vegetation, and split the clumps. They can then be given a good start in individual pots, before being planted out.

Cut the flower stems well before they reach maturity, tie them together in loose bunches and hang them head downwards in a cool moving airstream until they are dry.

This grass, also known as *Pennisetum longistylum*, forms a somewhat loose clump up to 30cm (2ft) tall with masses of more-or-less cylindrical flowerheads. They are up to half as wide as long, and can reach a length of 1.2cm (4in) with many long spreading bristles, some nearly as long as the heads themselves.

The plant is usually grown as an annual. Its seeds should be sown under glass in spring, and the young plants planted out when frost is over. In warm areas it could be sown where it is to flower, and thinned out to about 15cm (6in). Fertile well drained soil and full sunshine suit it best.

It can be dried easily, but should be cut well before maturity in order to minimize damage to the spikelets. Hang bunches of flower stem heads downwards in a dimly lit place and a current of cool moving air. This is a good subject for dyeing by the "dunkit" method.

Phalaris canariensis   CANARY GRASS

Phalaris arundinacea   REED CANARY GRASS

This grass and its smaller relative *Phalaris minor*, LESSER CANARY GRASS, are natives of the Mediterranean region. They are both tufted annuals, the larger growing up to 1.2m (4ft) high and the smaller up to 75cm (2½ft). *Phalaris canariensis* has an oval to egg-shaped flowerhead with spikelets up to 20cm (3in) long, green or purple, and developing into yellow seed which is used as food for pet birds, hence its name. *Phalaris minor* has a more cylindrical flower spike, with smaller spikelets and is less commonly grown.

Like most hardy annuals these species can be sown in mid-spring where they are to flower. They will grow in medium garden soil, like some sunshine, and should be thinned to about 10cm (4in) apart.

Cut the flower spikes when mature, and allow them to dry in a moving current of air. They can then be dyed by being immersed in a large container of florist's dye.

This is a wild grass found growing in marshy places. There is also a cultivated variety, *Phalaris arundinacea picta* (RIBBON GRASS or GARDENER'S GARTERS), which has longitudinally striped variegated leaves, and yet another variety, *Phalaris arundinacea luteopicta*, in which the variegation is yellow.

These grasses are very vigorous and grow up to 2m (6ft) high from spreading invasive rhizomes – a botanical way of saying that if you grow them in your garden, they're likely to take over everything about them, unless you trim their clumps by cutting them with a spade when they become too big for the place in which they're planted. They can be propagated by division, and are happy in moist garden soil.

Their flower spikes are up to 25cm (10in) long, somewhat coarse and irregular in shape, because of the alternation of groups of spikelets on different sides of the stem. Cut the grass with plenty of stem before the flowers are ripe and dry them carefully in a warm current of moving air.

Phleum pratense   TIMOTHY

Polypogon monspeliensis   ANNUAL BEARD GRASS

This is a somewhat tufted perennial grass which grows up to 1.5m (5ft) high and has cylindrical flowerheads, 15cm (6in), or sometimes longer. It grows wild throughout much of Great Britain, where it is cultivated as an important hay plant.

If you do, it should be sown in spring where it is to flower, in good garden soil. Or it can be propagated by division. Find someone who has a clump or go out and dig a piece from the nearest suitable wasteland. (This is not an encouragement to go round digging up wild plants). A small piece of Timothy will soon expand in your garden, and in the wild it is so widespread that a piece that size is hardly likely to be missed.

Cut the flower stems before they are too ripe, tie them up in loose bundles and allow them to dry, hanging head downwards in the dark and in a moving airstream. After that they can be dyed by the "dunkit" method.

Phleum alpinum   ALPINE CAT'S TAIL

A charming little grass, as its name suggests, *Phleum alpinum*, is a native of arctic and mountain regions. It grows up to 45cm (18in) high, with pointed leaves, and an oval flowerheads about 2.5cm (1in) long.

This is a plant for the rock garden where it should be grown in pockets of earth between the boulders, preferably in a somewhat elevated position. Use fairly light soil and sprinkle a few seeds into each site, thinning them when they have grown to a reasonable size.

Cut the flower stems, tie them in bunches and dry, head downwards in a moving air current. The heads can be dyed by the "dunkit" method and re-dried.

What a good name! Literally it means "many beards", and describes the robust flowerheads rather well. They can reach 15cm (6in) long by 5cm (2in) wide, with silky bristles, somewhat like a well-kept beard.

Annual Beard Grass is a native of Europe and Africa, though it has become naturalized in many other countries, including the United States, where it is known as "Rabbit Foot Grass".

It likes good light garden soil, and should be grown from seed, sown in spring, where the grass is to flower.

Secale cereale   RYE

Setaria italica   FOXTAIL MILLET

S. MONTANA

This used to be an important cereal crop but has largely been taken over by hardier strains of wheat. It survives in areas where a cold climate make it the only plant that can be grown. Otherwise wheat provides more useful grain for bread, while barley is more productive of animal feed.

Rye is a variable in height, from 30cm–2m (1–6ft). Its spikelets are held on a rather loose, sometimes wavy flowerhead. They have rough bristles or "awns" up to 5cm (2in) long, giving the flower spikes a coarse bristly appearance. Other related species, such as *Secale montana*, can also be grown for drying.

The plant may be grown as an annual or biennial, being sown either in spring where it is to flower, or in the autumn. It can make some growth until the ground freezes, and obtains a good growing start for the next spring. Rye likes free drainage, and is tolerant of both light soils and frost.

Cut the flower stems before they reach maturity, tie them in bunches and hang them, head downwards, in a moving current of air. When dry they can be dyed by the "dunkit" method. Throughout the drying and dyeing process, including the re-drying, take care with the long awns, as it is quite easy to damage them.

The seeds of this plant are used as food for pet birds. It grows up to 90cm (3ft) high, with very varied flower heads. According to variety, these are often up to 30cm (1ft) long, by 75cm (2½in) wide, with many bristles and drooping appearance, hence their name, from their resemblance to a fox's brush.

It can be grown in ordinary garden soil by being sown in spring where it is to flower, and it likes sunshine.

The spikes shed their spikelets easily, so must be cut for drying well before maturity, and dried carefully in a current of moving air. It may be advisable for this to be a warm current, because of the spike's bulk, but this could tend to make them "shed" more readily. It would also be a good idea to hang the spikes separately so that moving air has plenty of opportunity to reach them. These are factors with which you should experiment according to your own drying facilities, and the level of maturity at which you pick the spike.

After drying, the spikes can be dyed by the "dunkit" method. Once again take care to avoid dislodging the spikelets, especially when re-drying the heads.

Setaria verticillata ROUGH BRISTLE GRASS

Stipa pennata FEATHER GRASS

This annual grass has rather attractive "broken up" flower spikes, that is, the spikelets are grouped in little clumps along a straight axis, with distinct spaces between them. Their bristles (awns) do not all point in the same direction, and have fine sharp teeth on them.

This plant can be grown in a sunny spot, by sowing it in spring where it is to flower.

The flower spikes must be cut early, well before they reach maturity. Dry them by hanging them head downwards, in a current of moving air, then dye them if that is your fancy, by immersing them in a bath of dye until the colour has reached the intensity that you want, remove them, allowing them to drain, and drying them again. Take care during this process not to damage the flowerheads or spikelets.

Setaria glauca YELLOW BRISTLE GRASS

This annual grass has rather attractive "broken up" flower spikes, that is, the spikelets are grouped in little clumps along a straight axis, with distinct spaces between them. Their bristles (awns) do not all point in the same direction, and have fine sharp teeth on them.

This plant can be grown in a sunny spot, by sowing it in spring where it is to flower.

The flower spikes must be cut early, well before they reach maturity. Dry them by hanging them head downwards, in a current of moving air, then dye them if that is your fancy, by immersing them in a bath of dye until the colour has reached the intensity that you want, remove them, allowing them to drain, and drying them again. Take care during this process not to damage the flowerheads or spikelets.

This is a tufted decorative grass, whose flower heads look somewhat like multi-fingered inverted hands, with the fingers pointed upwards, and bent sideways. These "fingers", which are covered with fine hairs, are long bristles or awns growing from relatively few individual spikelets. When they dry they tend to curl into more of a claw shape, but are still most interesting to look at.

Stipa can be propagated by division, in early spring or autumn. Alternatively, seed may be sown in mid-spring, where the clumps are to flower, or under glass in early spring. In this case the seedlings should be allowed to grow on and planted out later. This plant likes a reasonably fertile garden soil and a well-drained position.

The flowerheads can be dried by being tied in loose bunches and hung head downwards in a current of dry moving air. Sometimes people dye them by the "dunkit" method but in our opinion they are interesting enough in their normal dried state for this to be unnecessary.

Tricholaena rosea   NATAL GRASS

Triticum aestivum   WHEAT

Also known as *Rhynchelytrum repens*, this grass grows up to 1.2m (4ft) high, and its feathery spikelets form a flowerhead up to 20cm (8in) long. As suggested by its English name, it is a native of South Africa. *Rosea* refers to the reddish colour of the spikelets.

In warm areas, *Tricholaena* can be sown in spring, where it is to flower, but generally gives better results if the seed is sown under glass, and the young grass planted out after frost danger is over. Alternatively, the plants can be kept in a cool greenhouse, in pots, to provide larger specimens. If they are grown outside, they need a sunny position and shelter from the wind.

Dry the flowers by hanging them head downwards in a current of moving air. They can be dyed by the "dunkit" method.

Wheat exists in a number of species and a large number of interbred varieties. *Triticum aestivum* is a bread wheat (other latin names are *Triticum durum* – MACARONI WHEAT, *Triticum turgidum* – RIVET WHEAT, *Triticum compactum* – CLUB WHEAT) and I have featured it here because it is the most common of the wheats.

You might collect a few flowering stalks before they are ripe, from a waste corner of a farmer's field, or a hedge bank. But please, *do not* pick plants from a growing field. These stems will vary in length according to variety, and nowadays, particularly where farming is highly mechanized, they are likely to be quite short.

Winter wheat is bred to be sown in late autumn and will not flower without being subjected to a cold spell. If you have just picked a head of wheat from a piece of waste ground, it will be difficult for you to tell whether it is winter or spring wheat – the latter is sown in spring and does not need the cold spell. Either you could double-up your sowings, sowing half your seed in each season, or you might like to try treating your grain to an artificial cold spell, placing it in the ice-box of your refrigerator for a few weeks. The best way to get the right seed is undoubtedly to ask a friendly farmer.

Wheat can be grown in a good loamy soil, with plenty of sunshine, and can be dried easily by being hung head downwards in a current of moving air. Pick it before the grains have filled out. Some people then dye the dried flower and stem, but we think it looks best in its normal golden glory. Long-stemmed varieties can be woven in and out of arrangements, or you can take up the craft of making decorative "corn dollies" with them.

This is a most important food crop especially in America and Africa. In poor parts of the world seeds are milled or crushed and made into bread or some form of porridge in richer parts – chiefly the USA – they are used as animal feedstuffs and ground to produce corn oil, sugar and syrup. The green crop is also used as animal forage, or for silage.

Having said all this, the average corn cob grown as a vegetable, or, in suitable climates, as a seed crop, is not a terribly decorative object. It's advisable for arranging to grow one of the ornamental maizes, such as *Zea mays japonica* or *Zea mays gracillima* which is even smaller only about 61cm (2ft) high. Both can be had as variegated varieties and plants are also available with cobs that have several different coloured grains. These are ideal for decorative purposes.

Sow the seed in a greenhouse, in early spring, and plant out later, avoiding frosts. Alternatively, in warmer areas at least, it can be sown in late spring where the plants are to grow. Allow a good spacing – 23–30cm (9–12in) for the smaller species – and make sure that at least some plants grow next door to each other, i.e., grow three or four rows in parallel, otherwise the flowers may not fertilize each other properly. It's also possible to grow plants in pots in a greenhouse.

For drying, allow the cobs to ripen well, cut them at whatever length suits you, possibly including some of the flamboyant leaves, and finish off in a warm dry airy place. Ideally it may be possible to stand the stems in a container, so allowing free circulation of air around the cobs and leaves.

FLOWER DRYING

There are essentially three methods of preserving flowers: using air, using a desiccant, and using glycerine. Each can be used in different ways to suit the different requirements of both plant and dryer. Air can be warm or cool, blown or naturally ventilated; desiccants can be sand, silica gel powder or a mixture of both; glycerine can be absorbed by a plant internally or externally (what we have described here as the "dunkit" method). There are no hard and fast rules to perfect home drying, but the guidelines we give here have proved successful for years, and will be a sound base from which to develop your own variations.

The Simple Method – Air Drying

The Principles

Perhaps the simplest way of drying any plant material is to hang it up and let the water evaporate from it. Gradually moisture passes from cell to cell within the material until it reaches the drier outside atmosphere. When the amount of water within the plant material has reached equilibrium with that in the atmosphere, the plant is as dry as it can be under those particular conditions.

This may seem rather theoretical for such a simple operation as flower drying. Far from it. To take another simple example, if the air outside the plant tissue is as moist as the inside of the tissue, the plant won't dry at all.

If this happens, other living things that flourish under wet conditions, such as moulds and mildews will begin to grow on the plant tissue. At best they will mark and discolour it. At worst they will rot it completely. And this process will go on for as long as there's enough moisture around to support the fungi to growing on the plant.

This is the reason that we must accelerate the drying of the plant tissue, because otherwise fungi, algae, bacteria and other small living organisms would find enough water in the plant cells to

1

2

continue living in them. You might then conclude that all you need to do is to make sure that the air outside the plant is drier than the inside of the plant itself. This is true, but it raises a number of questions.

First, how do you make sure that the air outside the flowers that you're drying is drier than the tissue inside them? Of course, if you pick a flower from the garden and put it in a centrally heated window, it will dry. But what happens if you put it into a warm, but damp airing cupboard? And in the first example, should you stand the flower in a glass of water or simply leave it lying on the window ledge?

Conditions

The simplest way of drying flowers is to hang them up in bunches and to allow the water to evaporate from them in the method described earlier. However, before going ahead with this, you must think about the best conditions.

First, the air outside the bunches need to be kept dry. There are three ways of doing this. Any moist air that surrounds the flowers as the water comes out of them can be moved away. In other words, you can make sure that a stream of air blows over the bunches, either by putting them near an open window or by using a fan or even the blower of a fan heater. It may also be possible to encourage air movement in a warm room by opening the top of a high window and allowing warm air to rise out through it. If, at the same time, another window at the far end of the room is also kept open to allow fresh air to enter, the circulating air will be encouraged to move across the drying flowers.

This current of moving air will encourage evaporation from the surface of the vegetation. To allow this to take place freely, flowers that are being dried in bunches must not be tied together too tightly. Keep them fairly loose so that moving air from outside the outside of the bunch will be able to penetrate the outer layers and, more important, moist air from the inside of the bunches will be able to diffuse outwards more readily to the point where it is blown away by the moving airstream.

Traditional drying methods suggest that the air used for plant drying should be cool air. It seems likely that the lone use of this method has arisen empirically, and doesn't reflect scientific study or any serious consideration of the factors that are needed, or even those most efficient for the process. As you'll see later, commercial dryers dry their plants in hot air, which they blow (or suck) through large rooms containing thousands of bunches. To a large extent this practice meets the commercial need to dry flowers quickly, and has been refined to make effective use of expensive equipment, such as blowers, drying racks and drying rooms ensuring that they are not tied up for longer than necessary (the average is about two days) per bunch of flowers dried. They succeed in turning out very acceptable bunches of dried flowers, "acceptable" that is to people such as you and me who buy them. They dry a lot of grasses that dry well under those conditions, those roses, for instance, are usually just opening from buds when dried, and can look rather wrinkled.

Flowers can only be dried as far as the

There are a variety of ways by which moisture may be encouraged out of plant material, and it is only by experience that you will work out for yourself which methods work best for you and the flowers you want to dry.

1 *Loosely tied bunches, hung up to benefit from natural ventilation of an open window.*

2 *Warm air inside is drawn up to a high level window. The bunches dry more quickly in the convection stream.*

3 *An artificially induced cool air stream speeds things up.*

4 *A fan heater on a time switch may be used in many ingenious ways.*

humidity of the air surrounding them allows. It is not possible for them to have a lower humidity than that of the air around them. In fact, it is probably not possible to remove *all* water from plant material however dry we may make the surrounding air, because some water is probably attached to the tissue chemically.

We can also see that dried plant material placed in air containing more moisture than the plants, will actually absorb water from the atmosphere. This is why even when dried your dried flowers will eventually grow mouldy if, for example, you keep them in a moist environment.

The conditions needed for successful air drying are that the air should be dry, warm and moving. I know that a lot of driers would argue with the second proviso because of the tradition that has grown up in flower drying of using cool air, but their flowers would dry more quickly (and this would help prevent damage from fungi and bacteria) if they used warm air.

Some might argue that using warm air increases the amount of fungal growth their drying flowers. One of the reasons for this is that people will insist on using warm, moist stagnant air. They stick their flowers in an oven or an airing cupboard – in the old days cottagers

used to use a warm kitchen, including a range with a kettle boiling on it continuously. This would be fine for growing African Violets but is no use at all for our purposes. They they wonder why they're enouraging mould to grow.

By the way, please don't try to grow African Violets in your airing cupboard; they need light as well as warm moist conditions.

Another source of confusion is that people often dry their flowers in warm light places, perhaps, for example, in a sunny window with a current of air blowing through a ventilator. Then the flowers fade and the heat gets blamed again. In this case it's not the heat but

Helichrysum stems do not stand up well to drying, so it is a good idea to cut the stems off (near right) *and to wire the flowers before hanging up the small bunches to dry* (above). *Helipterums, Everlasting Flowers, dry well on their own stems* (far right).

the light that's causing the trouble. To dry coloured flowers successfully, you must keep them dark because light will bleach the coloured pigments in the petals and cause them to fade, both while they are drying and afterwards. In other words, more quickly than if they had been kept in a darker part of the same room.

Hanging and Racking Space

The best way to dry flowers is in bunches. It is possible to dry them in racks on trays or shelves but flowers drying in this way tend to take up more room than those that have been tied up together and hung up in bunches. It also

involves more equipment, and if solid shelves are used it is not so easy to obtain free air circulation around the flowers.

The simplest way to dry flowers, and this is often the most successful despite its limitations, is to hang bunches of suitable flowers, head downwards, just beneath the roof of a potting shed. The sun's heat on black roofing felt above them provides a good source of warmth and, provided that at least two windows are left open to provide a through flow of air, any moisture will be carried away. If your potting shed is the type with relatively small windows and a steep pitched roof the drying flowers will also tend to be in dim light.

I have seen this system used successfully on a commercial scale for several thousand bunches per season of Limonium. (For a commercial grower, this is really a tiny turnover – big growers talk of tens of thousands of bunches per day – and Limonium or Statice, as it is commonly called, is a plant with papery flowers that dry easily). Even so, it shows that the method is efficient when used for suitable material. The "potting shed" in this case was vast, housing a tractor and trailer and all the other impedimenta of a horticultural enterprise, and having rows of cross beams that supported its roof, and were highly suitable as places to knock in nails and

If you are lucky enough to have a dark store room with good ventilation, your ceiling space will soon disappear as the summer harvest of Wheat, Poppy heads and Everlastings takes over.

hang the bunches. Even so, the flowers were receiving rather too much light and the system was heavy on labour, because all the bunches had to be lifted up above a person's head and taken down each time they were checked.

That problem is hardly likely to concern you, with the dozen or so bunches you are drying for the winter. However, you must take great care with light levels. It's all too tempting to hang your flowers in the roof of your greenhouse and leave it at that. If you do so, and provided that your greenhouse ventilators are wide open enough to encourage a flow of air, you may end up with a number of suitably dry specimens but they are likely to be unacceptably faded. This may not matter because you may be intending to dye the blooms anyway so you may well use the greenhouse like this for grasses. But even they will dry better (as will other species) with less fading and brittleness if you fit some sort of blind along your greenhouse roof, in order to reduce the light level.

Drying flowers in air can be inconvenient if you don't have some sort of garden accommodation such as a potting shed. You and yours may be prepared to abandon the airing cupboard for the cause of flower drying. In the same case, fit an extractor fan to the cupboard door, arrange a convenient entrance for fresh air and you will have a most suitable drying cabinet. A workshop, if it can be abandoned for a while, is also a good space if its windows can be blacked out and an air extractor fitted, and if you can run a fan heater there all night and day, you will then be able to dry flowers on a small commercial scale and sell them to defray some of the costs of electricity. But unfortunately, in my experience, such accommodating households are few and far between. There are alternatives.

As I've already hinted, any disused cupboard can be put to good use, especially if you can keep it warm with a time-controlled fan heater for some of the night. When flower drying, such heaters are the poor person's alternative to expensive horticultural equipment. I once managed to buy a tin cupboard complete with working heater and fan, from a second-hand auction. Apparently, it had been used in industry to dry wet clothing. It even had steel strips in the top of it to act as hanging places. And it was cheap. I believe it is still possible to buy second-hand tin cupboards without heaters. Perhaps you could cut a hole in the back of one to take the opening of a fan heater. If so, please be careful to put the heater on a time switch so that it is not switched on too long or too often, otherwise you may overheat the plant material. Worse still, you might cause a fire. Do be careful, too, with sharp edges of steel around the hole. It's also always possible to make a similar cabinet out of plywood and paint it in pretty colours.

The simplest possible drying space can be made from black plastic sheeting or bags. Acquire some stiff wire – old clothes hangers will do very well – cut and bend them into hoops and either twist the ends together or solder them together. Save one hanger for the top of the dryer and several with which to make cross pieces. Assemble a framework as illustrated here and cover it with black plastic, and stick the plastic onto the wire with sticky tape. Provided you leave the top and bottom open or make a series of vents or holes in both of them, air will naturally circulate through your dryer, particularly if you hang it over a radiator. (But be careful with gas or oil

With wire clothes hangers and a large, black heavy plastic bag you can make a useful portable drier.

heaters because not only do they give out moisture, which is bad for the flowers, they also tend to set fire to things). The cross wires will provide places to hang flowers and the whole contrivance will contain enough bunches for home decoration. It may even by possible to move a small dryer so that it can be hung over different sources of available heat such as radiators. One snag – they do become lopsided unless the load is hung very evenly.

If all this home construction work seems rather daunting, you could find a corner of a room with a radiator and hang thickish curtains across it. Or you could use a non-radiant heater to heat the air so that it rises up behind the curtain. As a precaution, place a spark-proof fireguard over it sufficiently far away from the heater to prevent any plant material falling onto it, overheating and catching fire. Even then it would be a good idea, in the interests of both economy and safety, not to run the heater continuously.

As for how to hang the bunches, traditionally they are hung head downwards. This came about probably because it's the easiest way. Stems tied together are naturally hung by the tying

An empty cupboard can be converted into a useful drying cabinet as long as a free flow of air can be organized – here a fan heater on a time switch and a high level vent.

point. On the other hand, it may have slightly more significance because hot rising air that is not being blown will reach the flowers while the air is at its driest, and therefore will absorb moisture from them more readily.

A small commercial drying shed is organized to dry a wide variety of flowers. The layout of the shelving presents some neat ideas for space saving.

A short loop of string put through an overhand knot as above can be tightened by pulling the top string as the stems shrink.

Some dried plants do not need to be bunched at all as (above), the Chinese Lantern. Statice, on the other hand, will bunch up well as long the bunches are loosely hung (right) to allow plenty of air to circulate.

Making the bunches

There are several ways of holding the bunches together. The only real difficulty is that, as the moisture evaporates from the flower stems, these tend to become smaller and slip through the fastenings. One obvious solution is to use elastic bands to hold the bunches together. In practice, these are difficult to fit over the fresh flower stems and, if not stretched sufficiently tight, will allow the stems to slip out as they dry.

Some people use wire and paper ties to hold the bunches. These are adequate provided the flowers are not too damp (encouraging mildew) and that the wires are long enough to fit around the fresh stems. Long wire ties as sold with dustbin liners seem to do this job quite well but I have not yet managed to find a way of buying them separately. These wires can be tightened up by being twisted as the flowers dry. They do tend to cut into the stems however, if they are twisted tight enough to hold them firmly.

Probably the best solution is also the most traditional one. Cut short lengths of string and knot them as shown here. Put the bunch of flowers through the loop you have formed with the knot and pull it tight. Then by knotting the two free ends of string you will have a loop by which to hang up your bunch. To tighten the string as the stems shrink while drying, all you need to do is to pull on the appropriate free end.

One final thing which is important for drying is to pick flower heads that are at the right stage of ripeness. Many grass heads for example, if allowed to ripen too much, will shatter on drying – i.e., the different parts of the flower will fall apart and you will be left with boring husks and leaves. Some flowers are best picked at the bud stage. Others can be left so long on the growing plant that they dry themselves. There are many differences between species and mention of it has been made under individual entries on the different plants.

Using a Drying Medium

Drying flowers in a current of warm moving air in a dark place is the traditional ideal. Grasses, for example, dry easily in this way, as do species such as Limonium. Other more delicate flowers are not so suitable. You can dry roses using this method, and commercial producers of dried flowers do so, but the result is not the glossy perfection that you might expect from this symbol of a June day. The reason is that rose petals are delicate plant tissue and drying them by such a simple method tends to make them curl and shrivel. Also, the base of a rose flower is thick and fleshy, much more so than the thin petals. To make it dry, more heat is needed, and a more prolonged period of drying than is required for the petals themselves. This increases the damage, and you cannot reduce the length of drying time to suit the petals without leaving the rest of the flower wet and liable to mildew.

The solution is to use a drying medium. This supports the petals while they are being dried, at the same time helping to extract moisture from them. There are several different drying agents, some of which are cheap and readily available, while others are more effective and more expensive.

Sand

The cheapest, most readily available drying agent is clean sand. Silver sand from a local pet shop, or builder's sand, is probably the easiest to come by. Sand from the beach is not recommended because it contains salt, and this will have a bad effect on specimens unless it is well washed.

Whichever source of sand you decide to use, it must be *very* clean. Place the sand in a container such as a plastic bucket and wash it thoroughly with clean water. Allow any debris to float to the surface and pour off the water. Repeat this a number of times until the water you are pouring off is absolutely clean. Then place the sand in a metal container and heat it in your oven at 120°C (250°F) until it is completely dry. Take it out and let it cool before using it. Alternatively, spread your sand on a clean cloth on the lawn or floor and let it dry in the sun or indoors.

The snag with using ordinary sand is that it will not absorb much moisture from plants before it has to be re-dried. The sand grains themselves absorb no water at all, because they are made of silica, an impervious and relatively chemically inert substance. What happens is that the water from the plant passes into the air spaces between the sand grains and from there diffuses between the grains until it escapes from the outside surface of the sand or through its container. Often this second stage takes place too slowly and the sand becomes saturated with water so that it has to be re-dried frequently. Also the sharp edges of some sand grains can cause a certain amount of damage to delicate plant tissues.

G. Condon in his book on flower drying *The Complete Book of Flower Preservation* recommends the use of a form of colithic sand obtainable from the Great Lakes area of the United States. This has rounded grains and contains a deposit of mineral salts which apparently help with the drying. People living in England near the Cotswold escarpment may like to try sand manufactured from the colithic limestone that can be found everywhere along this edge. This also has rounded grains and appears to have been laid down under similar conditions to the Great Lakes sandstone.

Wax and Sand

You could also try making a substance using wax and sand. Heat about 2.25kg (5lb) of sand in your oven until it is thoroughly dry and warm. Add one tablespoon of melted paraffin wax and stir very thoroughly so that all the grains receive an even coating. Allow the sand to cool and add one dessertspoon of fine silica gel. Mix again.

Borax and Sand

An old fashioned alternative is to use borax, or a borax and sand mixture, but this tends to attract insects to the drying flowers. Should you decide to try this, the ratio should be two parts of borax to one of sand. This gives an alkaline mixture which may suit some petals but tends to cake into lumps which do not make proper contact with the specimen. Some books recommend maize – or cornmeal, but this would have the same disadvantage.

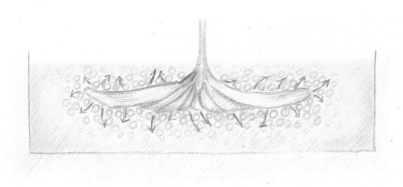

Sand grains do not actually absorb moisture; in the drying process the moisture is drawn away from the flower to the outside air, as shown by the arrows in the drawing.

Flowers can be dried face up or face down. Open flowers with strong petals are fine for drying face down using silica gel such as the Daisy (top). Flowers with delicate petals and more dense formation such as the Dahlia should be dried face upwards to avoid damage or distortion.

Silica Gel

The very best drying medium, although you will sometimes see it criticized on the grounds that it, too, has sharp particles and tends to dry the flowers too quickly, is silica gel. This is not to be confused with the silica in sand. It is a chemical that actually absorbs molecules of water (unlike the sand grains). This only happens when it is dry, and it goes on happening until the silica gel particles are saturated. They then have to be heated to drive off the water, when they can be used again and again. Silica gel is available with a chemical indicator which turns dark blue when completely dry, pale blue when somewhat wet, and pink when saturated, so it can be used to show the state of dryness in the silica gel. (For the chemically-minded, it consists of fine crystals of cobalt chloride). This is the ideal form to use for flower drying because you can tell when the silica gel needs re-drying, but not everyone bothers to use it.

Some people prefer to have already laid in a stock of plain white silica gel powder. However, whichever type you decide on, it must be a fine powder, the relatively coarse crystals which you can buy for drying photographic equipment and similar applications are useless. They will not form sufficiently close contact with the flower petals and are likely to cause localized scorching or over-rapid drying and distortion where they do touch the petals. This may be the reason why silica gel is still mistrusted by some flower dryers, yet I have seen complete open roses and complicated flowers such as passion flowers successfully dried by this method and subsequently embedded in polyester resin. This was done by an expert whose principal hobby in retirement was flower drying.

If you decide to use silica gel, it must always be stored in airtight containers which should be clearly labelled. Dry it by spreading it thinly over a clean baking tray and heating it in your own oven. Follow the manufacturer's instructions as to the correct temperature and always use a fine grade of powder.

Preparing the flower

You should not cut the flower until all your equipment is ready. The fresher the flower is before you start drying the better, and make sure that it is com-pletely dry. Any drops of water can be removed with a tissue, kitchen towel, or soft paint brush. The paint brush can also be used to position petals and anthers before drying.

It may be necessary to reinforce the point where the petals join the flower, and the best way to find out whether this needs doing is by experience. If you decide to reinforce, then a drop of diluted water-soluble glue or diluted clear nail varnish can be applied to the junction between petal and calyx with a small paint brush or an orange stick. The dilution should be one part glue to one part water, or one part clear nail varnish to one part nail varnish remover. The same glue or varnish can be used to stick the flower to an artificial stem.

Before you place the flower in the drying medium you must decide whether you are going to leave it on its natural stem or whether it would be better to dry the stem separately and replace it later, or put the flower on an artifical stem. It is often easier to dry a flower without its stem: the bloom takes up less space and artificial stems may look more attractive than wrinkled or faded natural ones. If you do decide to remove the natural stem, you should cut through it about 2.5cm (1in) away from the flower and push a pin into it. If you wish to use the natural stem you should push another pin into the centre of that, too, before drying it separately. Alternatively, you can use a short length of florist's wire. When the flower has been dried completely it is very easy either to replace it on its own stem or make up an artificial one for it.

To fit an artificial stem, remove the short length of florist's wire from the flower and glue in a length that corresponds to the length of stem you require. If you decide to use this method you should insert florist's wire into the natural, dried stem when appropriate, for the best effect. You can use either of the two glueing mixtures mentioned earlier. Occasional species, such as *Helichrysum*, exude their own glue from their cut stems in the form of sap, and shouldn't need anything extra. Allow the glue to dry, then stretch the florist's tape around the wire holding the tape and the wire at an angle of about 23–30° to each other, and then rotate the wire to get even coverage of tape as it runs down the stem. If you wish simply to replace the flower's natural stem, simply pull out the pin, glue it and put it back into its own hole, then cut off the pin's head and glue that end into the corresponding hole in the flower stem – like a dowel. You may find that the pin is already a tight fit in the stem. In that case, leave it. The same thing will happen with florist's wire. If is well worth collecting and drying other plant stems and using them as substitutes for the original ones. A pair of pliers or side cutters are very useful tools to have around when you are doing all this.

Supporting the flowers

There are a number of different ways of supporting flowers and foliage within the drying mixture. Which one you use will depend upon the flower shape, whether or not you wish to retain its stem, and the availability of suitable materials. Obviously these vary according to the species you're going to dry.

The method that requires the least equipment is the use of the drying material itself as a support for the flower. This is really only worth doing if the flower can be dried face downwards. For example, flowers of the daisy family could be dried by this method. The flower should be placed on a layer of the drying mixture and the mixture pushed up underneath it, care being taken not to displace the petals. Then the rest of the flower is covered, so that its petals are held from above an below by the mixture.

Flowers that have delicate anthers and stamens or curved or delicate petals need to be supported face upwards. it is not economical, convenient or necesary to do this by means of the drying mixture unless the flower has a stem that will not air-dry, i.e. a stem that needs to be surrounded by drying mixture. For these delicate plants you will need a thin stick, long enough to reach the bottom of the container. For short stems an orange stick would be ideal, for longer ones try using a split bamboo cane rounded at the ends – a stake for plant pots might be suitable.

Agitate the surface of the drying material with the chosen stick and as the material loosens, slide the plant stem into it. This will prevent your having to put too much pressure on stem and flower, and will avoid damaging them.

You will then have a flower whose head rests on top of the mixture and whose stem is buried in it. Then carefully pile more mixture around the flower, on top of it, and between its petals.

A more convenient method that will work on all flowers whose stems can be air-dried, is to support the flower, face upwards, near the top of the container. The support can be made of card, wire mesh or polystyrene sheet or block, depending upon the size and weight of the bloom to be dried. It is important to leave enough space above the support for the flower and drying agent. If you are using wire mesh, it will need to be covered with a sheet of paper to prevent the silica gel particles from falling down below the flower head. The best way to get the flow into the right place is to push its stem through a small hole in the paper. (Either make the hole with the stem itself, or some pointed object). Then place the paper on the wire mesh, making sure that the flower stem goes through one of the gaps. This can be quite awkward if you're trying to dry several flowers in the same container because it will be difficult to support them all while fitting them through the wire mesh. In this case, fit the paper to the wire and then make holes in it for the flower stems, or use polystyrene sheeting instead.

This method of supporting the flower heads is much more economical than trying to dry the flower in a deep mound of dessicant. Not only is less silica gel required but the flower can also be inserted more easily. And once a box has been fitted with this kind of support it can be saved and used over and over again.

Foliage, long flower spikes and flowers that are strongly asymmetrical like delphiniums, can best be dried in a horizontal position. The way to support them is to construct folded card ridges with slots cut in them, into which the stems fit. Both support and flower need to be surrounded by a suitable container. Either you can start collecting containers or you can make them yourself. For long specimens, boxes can easily be made by folding card and glueing the corners, or by taping strips of card together.

Applying the Medium

Once you have supported the flower,

The two cross sections above illustrate different methods of supporting a flower in containers. In both cases the stems are being air dried while the flowers are being dried using silica gel which is prevented from flowing down into the bottom half of the container by a shelf of wire netting covered with paper (top) or by a shelf made out of polystyrene (lower). The retaining rims, which can be made out of firm card or a deep cake ring, must be firmly taped to the supporting shelf, or the fine silica gel will escape. The rims should be tall enough to take a good 1cm ($\frac{1}{2}$in) of gel above a covered flower.

you must cover it with drying mixture. This requires great care if the petals and other parts are to remain in their natural positions. Cup your hand and fill the palm with a comfortable amount of the drying mixture. Then curl your fingers over it. This will enable a small trickle of the mixture to be poured out of the side of your hand furthest from the thumb. The stream of sand can be varied by opening or closing your fingers, so that the space between palm and little finger becomes bigger or smaller. This speed of flow of the material can be varied by tilting your palm more or less. There should be about 2.5cm (1in) of free space around each flower to be dried.

If you are using any kind of sand, without silica gel, it is important to make sure that the surface area of the exposed drying material is large in proportion to the volume of the container. In other words, containers should be relatively flat or short, rather than long and narrow. This is another reason for using solid supports of polystyrene or card because these allow a low volume to surface area so that moisture can escape from the sand more readily. This only applies to sand because in this case the water vapour from the drying specimen has to escape into the surrounding air.

If you are using silica gel on its own or a gel and sand mixture the ratio of volume to surface area does not much matter since the silica gel absorbs the water. With complicated or delicate flowers it might be better to dry one flower to a container, at least until you gain experience, otherwise you may damage adjacent specimens when you are either covering or uncovering one of them.

If the flower is being supported face down directly on the drying material, put a layer of about 1.25cm ($\frac{1}{2}$in) deep in the bottom of the container. Place the container on an old tablecloth or sheets of newspaper so that any spilt drying medium can easily be poured back into the storage box or jar. Perhaps the easiest way of doing this is to stand the container in a large, quite shallow cardboard box, which will be rigid enough to allow loose grains to be poured easily.

With the flower in position, pour the drying material gently around it using a small paint brush to position the flower parts and making sure that the material falls evenly on all sides. Otherwise it may be distorted. Long spikes processed in an upright container will need to be held upright while the material trickles in between the florets. It may be necessary to cut off florets and dry them separately from the stem, rejoining them later (with glue and florist's wire). This is particularly necessary if the florets and stem are of very different thicknesses, otherwise one or the other will dry too quickly.

When the container is full, tap its side gently to eliminate any air pockets and top up the mixture if necessary. Make sure you label all containers with the name of the flower, the date and, if it varies, the kind of mixture you are using. If you are using silica gel, it is a good idea to enclose the whole container in a polythene bag. Next you will need patience. Try not to remove any mixture until you are fairly certain that the flower has dried. Drying times can vary from 3 to 4 days to 3 weeks, depending upon the species and the kind of drying compound you are using. The shorter times are for pure silica gel and/or relatively dry specimens; the longer ones are for fleshy specimens and/or pure sand. To check whether a flower is dry, turn the container sideways and gently tap off some of the mixture into another container until you have exposed some part of a petal. This should feel nicely dry, but not so dry as to be brittle. If it seems right, continue tapping and pouring until the whole specimen is exposed. Under no circumstances try to pull a

The heads of flowers can be held in position by a simply made rack of folded and notched card. The long spikes of Delphinium (below) are more satisfactorily dried horizontally with the stem held in the notch so that it can't move sideways as the gel is poured over it.

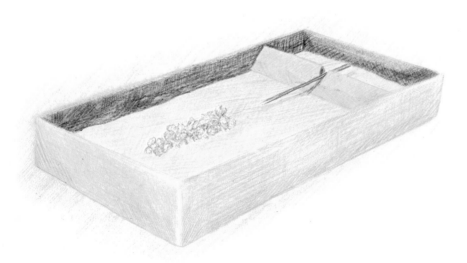

dried flower out of the drying medium or you will probably break it. You may have to use a paint brush to remove the final few grains from between the petals.

Dry your silica gel by heating it and storing it in an airtight jar, clearly labelled. Apart from a little wastage, this expensive medium will last a long time. Take comfort from the fact that almost all the rest of your equipment for this method can be home-made quite cheaply.

It is a good idea to enclose the finished box in a polythene bag to prevent atmospheric moisture being absorbed by the gel.

When emptying the silica gel out of the box after the flowers are quite dry, have a large sheet of newspaper or cardboard box on top of your work area to stop the gel from going all over the place. A gentle tapping motion to the side of the box should allow the gel to flow away without disturbing the flowers.

Preserving with Glycerine

Powdery substances such as silica gel are not the only way of preserving plant material. Long pieces of vegetation, such as beech twigs, would be very difficult to preserve in this way. You would need an extremely large container and a large quantity of silica gel to make the process possible. Failing this you would need a separate container for each group of leaves, which would be extremely fiddly, and the weight of the container could probably break off as many twigs as dried. Besides, it would be almost impossible to dry the twigs at all using this method, because water would not diffuse out of them fast enough to be readily removed.

A better way is to put a preservative *inside* the plant. This then rises up the twigs, preserving them, and ends up in the leaves. Fortunately, as anyone who has taken elementary biology lessons at school will know, this is extremely easy to do, at least in principle.

Living plants take up water all the time, partly by the action of their roots – this is called "root pressure" – and partly be evaporation from their leaves, leaving a deficit of water which is supplied through the stems and twigs below them. When we're preserving cut plants we don't have any root pressure and our efforts have to rely on the evaporation of water from the leaf surfaces. This is quite enough. It is possible to make dyes rise up cut twigs and into the leaves of bushes such as laurel simply by placing the twig in a glass of diluted dye. This is exactly the way in which we preserve them, except that instead of dye, we use a liquid – the commonest one is glycerine – which will rise up inside the tissues and prevent fungi and bacteria from being able to live on them.

The glycerine is always mixed with water and, although one-to-one proportions are used by some people, this seems unnecessarily expensive, and for most

purposes one part of glycerine to two of water will be quite adequate. If you find the preserved foliage starts to grow mould or fungi, try a more concentrated solution. Foliage is the main part of a plant to be preserved in this way, although just for the sake of experiment it might be worth trying some of the bigger harder stemmed flowers such as Larkspur.

In order to make it easier to mix the glycerine with the water, the water should be very hot, just off boiling, and the mixture should be stirred well and allowed to cool. It is most important to cool it to below at least 38°C (100°F) before placing plant tissue in it, because plant cells are killed at temperatures not much higher than that Sometimes you are advised to hammer the ends of the stems, but we think this is not a good idea as it does seriously damage the plant cells. Instead, we would advise you to use a sharp knife and cut the stems diagonally immediately before putting them into the glycerine mixture. This avoids damage to all but a thin layer of cells along the cut, helps to expose cells to the liquid, and removes any cells that may have become full of air. In some flowers which are to be preserved in this way, for example *Molucella*, you have to be quick and plunge the cut stem into the glycerine mixture as soon as it has been cut from the living plant. This is a technique well worth remembering if you are having trouble.

The stems should be left standing in the mixture until all the leaves have absorbed it. This will be obvious by a change of colour or texture in the leaves. To encourage rapid uptake of liquid it's best to have moving air passing over the leaf surface. Some people also advise you to keep them in the dark, perhaps to avoid fading, but we're not sure that this is of any real advantage.

It may well be that you will have difficulty in preserving foliage in this way if the leaves are unusually leathery or the whole stem is too long – say more than 30cm (1ft) to 45cm (18in) high. Either the surface of the leaf may be too tough to allow evaporation or the stem may be too long for what evaporation there is to be able to lift water that high. A different method is to lay the twigs down in a bath of glycerine mixture – in this case two parts of glycerine to one of water will be better – and allow the

Foliage is best preserved either by standing upright with stems in a mixture of glycerine and water which it will draw up into its leaves. Or the foliage can be preserved in a "bath" of the mixture – the "dunk-it" method – when small pebbles may be needed to hold the leaves under the surface.

liquid to soak into them. The glycerine should be prepared as described above, but the plant should be removed from it when about two-thirds to three-quarters of each leaf has darkened or changed colour. You will probably have to hold the foliage under the surface of the glycerine, and this can be done by using small weights such as pebbles. After it has absorbed enough liquid, wash the plant with a little soapy water, rinse it with fresh water and allow it to dry, otherwise it may be too floppy for good flower arranging. This drying may also be necessary for plants preserved in glycerine by the "upright method". Their leaves sometimes exude drops of glycerine, which should be wiped off first.

In a few special cases, such as *Molucella*, the plant really does need a thorough course of air drying after its

Dyeing dried Plants

relative to glycerine, it is poisonous and can be corrosive as any of you unfortunate enough to have spilt it on your car's paintwork will undoubtedly know. *So, treat it with care.* The glycol should be mixed with water. This is an experimental method so try two parts of glycol to one of water for a start, but be prepared to decrease the proportions to three or even four to one in order to achieve the correct balance.

The main feature of this method is that it can produce marked colour changes in the plants. It also has the advantage that glycol is cheaper and more readily available than quantities of glycerine.

People who preserve foliage using the glycerine method often make mixed arrangements with fresh flowers, and here, the bottom of the preserved foliage stems should be blocked by being dipped into molten wax or smeared with it so that water can't seep easily into the dried or preserved stem.

You can deliberately dye your plants and, with practice, you can produce the colours of your choice, rather than the more random ones produced by glycol. Your choices of method are the same as when using glycerine: either the "dunk-it" method, or what we have called "the upright" method which is what a biologist would call a systemic method because the dyes or the glycerine are taken up into the plant's interior. This method is not quite so accurate as the dunk-it method (generally used on pre-dried material) because chemical reactions between the dyes and the plant tissues may produce colours that are not intended.

For coarse woody plants you could try using wood dyes, which should be water soluble, but special florist's dyes are really more suitable. For the systemic method you could even use coloured Indian inks, so try using lots of vivid colours. For the dunk-it method – and this is the one usually used with grasses, the grasses being dried first and then dyed – florist's dyes are probably best, but you can experiment with ordinary household dyes, and don't use the ones that require boiling.

All plants that have been dyed need drying afterwards or redrying in the case of those which were dried first then dyed by dunk-it, and great care should be taken during this second drying to make sure that the flowers aren't damaged. This is especially true for grasses, which have an annoying habit of shedding the parts of their flowers (shattering) if they aren't handled carefully. All dried or preserved flowers should be kept in a dry atmosphere, otherwise they will absorb moisture and fungi and bacteria will be able to live on them.

treatment with glycerine, so that the whole process becomes more of a cross between glycerine treatment and air-drying, but this is a specialized way of doing things, more important to the commercial flower dryer.

The colour of the foliage remains more or less the same after preservation in glycerine. Some leaves do change colour completely; for instance, magnolia turns dark brown, beech turns brown, and broom almost black. The leaves, however, do stay nice and flexible rather than becoming brittle. This is an advantage of the method.

There is a more experimental substance that has been used with a fair degree of success. This is glycol, the chemical found in car antifreeze. Strictly, it should be called ethylene glycol and, although it is a close chemical

Commercial Drying

Selling dried flowers is a big and fast growing business. Dutch growers produce hundreds of thousands of bunches a week for export and, although the individual companies have each developed slightly different processes they all dry their flowers within a two to three day time scale using hot moving air. This is heated to 60°C (140°F) and then passed through huge drying rooms containing large chambers of wheeled metal racks on which the flowers are hung. The same method is used on a smaller scale in England, where flowers are hung in bunches on wooden racks in just the way that was described earlier in this book. Air is then blown through the large darkened room containing the racks, and only in damp or colder weather is it first passed over a heater. This is a somewhat slower method than those used in Holland because on the whole cooler air was being used, but nonetheless it worked well.

It is possible to pre-dry air by passing it over trays of silica gel but, except on a small scale, the cost of the drying agents is prohibitively high. I was asked in 1984 to advise a commercial dryer whether or not he should pre-dry the air going into his drying chambers, using large trays of silica gel, which could be re-heated once the air had been dried. The reason for this was that his proposed plant was to be sited in a place that had a damp atmosphere and he was worried whether the air going into his drying sheds would be sufficiently dry. The cost then of the silica gel *alone* without any ancillary equipment was about $9,000 (£6,000) and this was for enough to dry only one tonne of fresh flowers, and at 1984 prices. Another that was discussed was that of pre-cooling moist air in order to remove some of the moisture from it before heating it and passing it over the flowers in the usual way. What we found was that this double process used on air of 70 percent relative humidity at 21°C (70°F) and cooling it to 4.5°C (40°F) before re-heating to 60°C (140°F), used 35 per cent more energy and removed only 4 percent more moisture than heating the air directly from 21° to 60°C (70° to 140°F).

This does not, however, totally invalidate the use of refrigeration in flower drying. Freeze drying, for example, is a well-known process in which water is removed from substances such as meat by being 'sublimated'', that is, removed as solid particles while the meat is at low temperature and under high vacuum. This avoids damage to the tissue and obviously has fascinating possibilities for plant drying. It has been tried on individual blooms but the equipment is extremely expensive, costing thousands of pounds for a space big enough to dry ·03m³ (1ft³) of plant material. The reason that it's expensive is that it uses high vacuum and low temperatures simultaneously and, while this can be justified with something such as sliced beans, where a ·03m³ (1ft³) chamber holds quite a large number of beans, only one dahlia, for example, would fit into that space and there would still be a problem of handling, because beans can be tipped in and out mechanically while flowers can't. Up till now, so far as I know, this method has not been used commercially.

It may be that blast freezing, where very cold air is blown across fresh

A large commercial drying chamber (above) *will be filled with racks each holding hundreds of bunches of flowers for drying. On a less ambitious level it is possible to adapt a commercial kitchen oven to do the job very successfully* (right).

At the Star factory in Holland, the freshly picked flowers are brought in daily by individual growers (above). *Teams of students sort and bunch the flowers* (right) *in their summer vacation, which is the high season for all flower dryers. The bunches are then hung on wheeled racks* (over right) *awaiting their turn in the huge drying chambers where they will be checked regularly until they are fully dry.*

material in order to evaporate water from it by the same process of sublimation, may in the long run prove more useful. The cold air can be salvaged and re-circulated and this process is already being used for more items such as seafood.

But these ideas are merely speculative, and even if they do become practical ways of drying flowers, their expense will mean that they are used only by big commercial dryers. On a smaller scale there is a commercial practice that may be more useful, namely the use of drying ovens. These are large and electrically heated to discourage the formation of water vapour, and contain a fan that draws fresh air through the oven and remove damp air. Sometimes they are adaptations of ordinary commercial kitchen ovens. I have seen excellent specimens of *Helichrysum* produced in this way, the flowers being placed in a pretty tough species, which doesn't fade much, and the process was being used to hasten its drying, but there's scope for experiment here. On a home scale you might

try an oven fitted with a fan. An adapted electric cooker could be suitable to keep the air in it from becoming stagnant although this is a more ambitious project than the tin cupboard previously mentioned.

Make sure that you have all electrical work carried out by a properly qualified electrician otherwise there is a chance that you and your drying area could end up over dried in a plume of blue smoke.

ARRANGING

The different textures, the subtle tones of colour, the varied plant profiles all contribute to the satisfaction dried and preserved plant material give to the flower arranger. Some dried flowers are very delicate and need careful handling and artificial support, others will withstand quite tough treatment. But, perhaps, what arrangers enjoy the most is the limitless range of different colour effects and shapes that can be created from informal to formal posies, from ropes and garlands to great standing arrangements; all of which last and last.

The ideas and practical tips on techniques and materials here will, we believe, provide the inspirations for individual creativity even for the beginner.

Tools and equipment

Tools and equipment. Left to right: *serrated knife, florist's wire, wire snips, secateurs, florist's scissors, pointed scissors, stretchy florist's tape, ribbons, and assorted foam shapes.*

Once you have your bundles of dried flowers waiting to be used, the next stage is to get equipped with a few simple tools and materials to help with making up the flowers into arrangements, or whatever you choose to do with them. Most of the things needed can be bought in florist shops and special departments in large stores, but sometimes it is worth buying certain things, such as wire, wholesale from a florist's merchant rather than in small packs of 20 or so at a time.

An essential tool to start with is a good pair of secateurs for cutting all types of plant material. Keep them as sharp as you dare and don't be tempted to use them round the house and garden for odd jobs. Secateurs should not be used for wire cutting unless they are specially designed to do so, and, as you may need to cut wire often, invest in a pair of wire cutters or some snips designed to cut wire, paper, plants, string and anything else you may come up against. A small fine pair of scissors with pointed ends are also useful for delicate trimming of flowers and cutting fine string or thread.

A long-bladed knife is handy for cutting expanded foam but the blade doesn't need to be very sharp and you could make do with an old, worn-out bread knife, for example. A serrated edge seems to work particularly well, Don't bother to buy new when you can use something you already have.

For many projects you will need the special expanded foam which is sold for dried flower arrangements. This is used *dry*, unlike the soakable type used for fresh flowers, and it is normally a neutral grey/brown colour which is easily hidden among stems and stalks. Light and bulky, it can be used over and over again until too riddled with holes to hold together. Expanded foam is available in basic rectangles and specialized shapes such as spheres and cones for making balls and pyramids. You can, of course, cut shapes yourself and join pieces together with tape or wire to make whatever foundation you need.

Wires of some kind will need to be used on occasion either at the drying stage or later in an arrangement. Many flowers don't have strong enough stems after the drying process to hold their heavy heads upright; and Helichrysums have to be wired straight after picking and then left to dry. (The sap from the heads of the flowers in effect rusts like glue onto the wire and are thus held permanently in place). Wires come in different thicknesses and lengths and are usually sold by weight from wholesalers or in small bundles from florist shops. If you are buying only one size of wire to begin with go for a long one, as it can always be cut shorter, but make sure it is a thick enough gauge for all the jobs you may need to do. The steel wires normally sold for floristry work rust very easily, so store them somewhere dry wrapped in a piece of oiled paper or in a plastic bag. If allowed to rust too far they are useless.

Fine pliable rose wire is excellent for tying and attaching small pieces of work. Usually sold on a roll, it is brightly silvered, and is easier to use than thread because it can be twisted or tied virtually with one hand, and it stays where you put it. Use it for all kinds of jobs because it is clean and neat and, being so fine, hardly shows on the finished work.

You may need a roll of special sticky tape suitable for fixing foam to containers or foam to foam, and sometimes stems need rolling in tape, too. Buy this tape from a florist shop. Ordinary tape sold for sticking paper together will not do.

Apart from the basic tools and equipment listed here, there is little else needed until you graduate to rather specialized arrangements.

If you are using your flowers in straightforward designs: standing in vases, jugs or baskets for example, then don't leave it too late to check you have a suitable range of containers to ensure plenty of choice and freedom.

Preparing the flowers

Many of the flowers you choose will need nothing more doing to them once they are dried. Some that have been dried in a dessicant may have been wired as described earlier in the book. Other types such as Helichrysums, which have very weak stems, must be wired before drying, and once dried are ready for use. Small or delicate flowers should be handled as little as possible and used just as they are. Others such as Larkspur, have lovely strong stiff stems, although the flowers can be very brittle and inclined to fall off if not wired on to the stem. A few subjects such as *Scabiosa Stellata* may hold together better if given a quick spray of fixative such as hair-

spray, but avoid shiny lacquers and anything that has a nasty unnatural look. The way to prevent seed heads and certain flowers from losing their petals or seeds is to choose the time of harvest so as to catch things at exactly the right point. If taken too soon, they never properly open out; too late, and they drop. Clematis is an example where the fluffy seed heads have to be picked while they are still silky and not yet turning to the fluffy stage. This turning is best learnt from experience over the years. Summer weather can make a big difference, too, to the quality and colour of flowers. There are definitely good and bad seasons for various plants. Dull, above average rain-fall summers produce sappy, soggy plants which, although dryable, are never as good as those that have enjoyed high sunshine quotas and low humidity. But then Hydrangeas love a wet season, so there is no suiting every plant.

If you have a large collection of homegrown dried flowers you may well not want to use them all straight away but to store them for later use. You can keep them for long periods either hang-

ing in the bunches they were dried in somewhere dark and clean, or laid gently in boxes such as shoe boxes with lids, or in long roomy boxes of the type used by flower growers to despatch goods to market. Once in boxes, flowers take up less room than hanging because you can stack them in layers; but they can also get damaged stored in this way and it isn't ideal for fragile varieties. If you need to keep them stored out of the way for a few weeks then simply stand bunches of single varieties in baskets or tall containers and put them where you will get the benefit of them straight away. For short-term storage this is fine, and they shouldn't fade or get too dirty over several weeks. Glycerine-preserved foliage is best stored wrapped with waxed or greaseproof paper, either flat in boxes or rolled in bunches, and then kept upright or hanging from a hook or beam. Keep well away from furnishings to avoid staining from the glycerine.

Wiring

Often small bunches of flowers such as Cornflowers need to be wired together to be used in larger areas than single heads would provide. This is a good way to avoid spotty arrangements and to get solid blocks of colour when needed. Simply bunch several stems together around a stiff wire. Hook the end of the wire around the stems under the flowers, being careful not to snap off the heads in the process. Wrap fine rose wire round the stems and then use the bunch as you like.

Larger flowerheads, such as Hydrangeas and Achilleas, often need to be split up into smaller pieces. After picking off some of the florets you will be left with one piece on the original stem and lots of loose pieces without a stem. Depending on the solidity of the base of the petals, either push a wire into it or hook an end through in some way so that it can be bound in place with rose wire. Keep any spare odds and ends from this splitting up and store bits of flowers for other arrangements or bowls of loose petals, or to add colour to pot-pourri.

Sometimes more than one wire may be necessary for a really heavy flower or as a means of securing an awkward part of an arrangement.

Small flowers should be wired together in clusters. Break off several flowers with a small amount of stem, attach them onto a single stiff wire and finish with florist's tape.

Containers

For any arrangement of flowers, fresh or dried, the container that holds them is always more than just a support. It is vitally important in a visual sense as well as in a practical one. For a dried arrangement the container doesn't always have to have a really firm base and it needn't hold water. But there must be enough weight for a top-heavy group of dried flowers not to keep toppling over when brushed against or caught in a draught. Any lack of stability can easily be solved with a few heavy stones or some sand put at the bottom of the container, or the use of one of those lead pin flower holders. Old cracked china, baskets, and wooden containers can all be used for dried flowers because there is no water involved and there is a chance to use far more complicated and difficult shaped containers than would be possible in a fresh arrangement.

Dried flowers have a very special quality of their own and a subtlety that is easily lost by combining them with unsympathetic materials. Their softness and simplicity fights with the bright hard surface of glass where the shine and transparency is at odds with the dull texture of most dried flowers. Pale milky opaque glass in pastel shades might look good with some careful colour scheming but the transparent kind is best avoided. The only time it does look good is when a plain glass shape, such as a large round bowl or simple square tank, is layered up with loose petals in a sort of visual potpourri.

China vases, jugs and bowls in strong simple shapes can work well, ranging from rough brown earthenware to elegant 18th century pieces. Colour and shape are the details to watch for and steer away from anything too fussy and pretty in the way of pattern that might fight with the flowers themselves. Pale or strong colours look good, but plain white china, while looking stunning with the vivid colours of fresh flowers, looks too cool and stark with dried ones. Tiny all-over designs on china have a homeliness that suits the arrangements well, and lustre glazes in all colours look marvellous with the paler colours found in many dried flowers. If you don't possess much suitable china, then ordinary terracotta garden plant pots look superb

with many arrangements, and everyday kitchen jugs have the relaxed style that is part and parcel of most dried flower arrangements.

Bowls, jugs and old preserving pans and saucepans made from copper and brass go wonderfully well with dried flowers. Old pieces look best after they have mellowed and acquired the right patina and occasional dents, but new vessels are also fine, and unless heavily laquered, will age with grace and start to look even better. Pewter, too, has the

right kind of sheen and depth of colour that suits dried things; but silver has the same chilly quality as glass, and somehow doesn't ever look right.

Dried flowers in baskets have almost become a design cliché, but there is no doubt that their popularity has come about because the two work so well together. Their texture and feel are similar, and often their colours are too. Old baskets are great favourites particularly some of the old painted and now faded florists' baskets. You can recreate this look by spraying with pastel coloured car paint and wiping over the surface slightly to remove some of the paint, leaving a two-toned effect. The choice of new baskets is huge these days, and they come in wonderful shapes, tiny ones for miniature posies, great round fruit-picking baskets, and the humble bicycle basket, which is a great shape for a dried arrangement. Another natural material that looks right with dried flowers is wood. It is rarer to find bowls and dishes in wood than in other materials but they do exist, even if you have to raid the kitchen for a salad bowl or part of a mortar and pestle set.

It is easier to start with a container and then choose flowers to fill it, rather than the other way round, but whichever choice you have to make, never underestimate the importance of the container you stand the flowers in.

Far left *The texture and colour of basketware has a natural affinity with all dried flowers. Here a glossy new basket has the richness needed to show off the brilliant colours of Helichrysum and the sheen of Honesty seed pods.*

Left *You will need containers of every shape and size, so search for old or antique bowls and jugs as well as new ones. A roomy woven basket designed for waste paper makes the perfect informal home for generous bunches simply arranged.*

Above *Natural earth textures and colours always look good with dried flowers. Handthrown and beautifully irregular terracotta flower pots make perfect containers and the drainage hole doesn't matter. The gilded fluffy seed heads of Clematis stand happily alongside a posy of pink Acrolinium.*

Colour scheming

Planning an arrangement for a particular place in a room means you will have a good idea of the colours you wish to use before putting everything together. Faced with a bundle of flowers of every type and colour and a free hand in how to use them, the best way to start is to grade them into various colours and see which looks good with which by holding them against each other and summing up the results. Bright mixtures of strong colours combining reds, yellows, oranges through to blues can work well if you have the confidence. There is something about the richness of dried flower colours, even the bright ones, that gives a glow, reminiscent of the colours of oriental rugs.

A scheme based on one or perhaps two basic colours and all shades between is a bit safer however. A mix of rusts, reds and terracottas through to peach and coral could work well, or you could try an even subtler combination of greys, greens and pale smoky blues in equal tonal values. Arrangements based on strong contrasting colours such as yellow and purple might just come off but could easily look harsh and synthetic. A tried and trusted colour scheme based on creams and faded straw colours is nearly always successful, especially if there are some strong shapes and outlines in the mixture and perhaps some soft feathery outlines such as grasses. This scheme has the added advantage of retaining for a long time the colours it started out with, unlike many flower colours that fade in strong light. Varieties do not fade at the same rate as each other, but even in an arrangement with dozens of different plants, what seems to happen is that they slowly age together and then over a period of time simply evolve into a slightly different arrangement.

After a period of time, take the whole thing apart and sort through the flowers, keeping any that still look fresh and re-usable, and discarding those that are too dirty and faded. With the addition of some totally new flowers you can often revive an elderly arrangement for several more months.

Above *A brave and unexpected colour mix which really pays off. The starting point came from the enamel painted jug and chair and led on to a startling combination of purple, yellow and cerise statice.*

Right *A gentle back-lit arrangement on a country window sill. The hot pinks of Acrolinium flowers are toned down with plenty of light and airy cream and silver.*

Top *Using all the natural bleached and brown colours in colour scheming made easy. Subtlety comes from tone variations and the many textures.*

Left *A rich tapestry effect is achieved using strong but subtle purples, blues and rusts like an ancient wall hanging. Bunches are simply tied to a painted trellis.*

Right *A splash of white highlights the mixed pinks in this arrangement.*

Placing dried flower arrangements in front of direct light is not generally successful – you lose the colour. However, the hazy silhouettes created by thistle heads and grasses can be very effective. The "cottage" look of casually hung bunches is also appealing.

Finishing Touches

Lighting and Positioning

Dried flowers lose the translucency of fresh petals, so their positioning in relation to a light source is very important. If you stand a dried arrangement in front of a light source such as a window, then the shapes of the flowers are thrown into relief but the colour is lost. This would be fine for an arrangement using thistle heads or grasses, where the outlines are all important. When colour is the important part of an arrangement, however, make sure of a solid plainish background and light coming from above or from a spot, or from the front and/or sides.

It pays to experiment with lighting to get maximum impact and drama from flowers, remembering that colours very often change in artificial light. They become either richer and more intense or sometimes fade and bleach away to a mere hint of their former strength.

Cleaning

Removing dust from dried flowers is not easy, and any that are too dirty are best thrown away. Some are tough enough to withstand a really good shaking outside in the fresh air, but many will be far too fragile for this kind of treatment. A gentle blow or a going-over with a soft brush to remove obvious surface dust will help, but you cannot dunk the whole thing in water or vacuum clean it without ruining the flowers.

It is tempting to think that because the flowers are dried they will last for ever. Nothing looks sadder than a very old dusty arrangement collecting cobwebs in a corner or high up on a forgotten shelf. Be strict and check your flowers often, and be prepared to remake them or throw them away if they are past their best.

Arranging – The First Steps

Too much advice on technique can put off the most enthusiastic person. There are no definite rules here that have to be adhered to. You just need a certain amount of confidence and a very few basic guidelines and principles. If you want to learn how to arrange flowers in a structured and more formal way you should find out about what classes are available locally.

If you are new to using dried flowers but have some experience of arranging fresh flowers, then there are a few differences between the two worth noting. Dried flowers are very definitely dead, stiff, and straight, without any of the relaxed curvy shapes found in cut flowers. In an arrangement, dried flowers stay still and static; they will not open out or move or bend to the light in the way fresh flowers do. The stems are never beautiful and generally need to be hidden and because only a few dried leaves look good, the flowers become all important. In a fresh arrangement it is possible to make something beautiful using very little material – perhaps just one or two perfect blooms and a little foliage, but with dried flowers you will need plenty of the basic ingredients to make the arrangement full and abundant.

Before beginning an arrangement, gather everything you will need and give yourself plenty of space to work in. Some flowers make lots of mess – so be prepared. Having more plant material than you need is much better than having too little, so be generous. It's amazing how dried flower arrangements swallow up flowers. If possible, work on an arrangement at the same height as the finished piece will be, or better still, work in the actual place. Choose whether the arrangement is to be viewed from one direction, from all round, or from above, such as in the case of a low, wide coffee table-top arrange-

ment. Fix foam into the container and tape it firmly and as invisibly as you can. If you are using very thick or heavy stems you may need to put a piece of fine mesh or slightly crumpled wire netting over the foam, fastening it to the container with wire. This measure often helps to support the arrangement and to keep it stable.

In each bunch of flowers you have chosen there are probably some special ones, some that are more ordinary, and perhaps plenty of filling-in material for finishing off. If you sort things out in this way in your mind's eye before you start, it will give you an idea as to how things should progress. If you want a dense and abundant look, which invariably makes the flowers look their best, then use groups of one colour and variety in small bunches rather than individual

The possibilities for arrangements are endless as this charming combination of styles shown above proves. Always have plenty of material to hand as it is surprising how much you will need.

stems. In this way you build up areas of colour and texture that can be merged into each other, graduating the colours as you move across the arrangement. Single flowers dotted about result in a spotty and incoherent colour scheme that is only successful when there is lots of space around each flower, such as you might find in a grouping of fresh flowers. Putting bunches together in this way works extremely well when the surface is on one plane, but it can also be used for arrangements where the flowers have different lengths of stem. The flatter, all-

Your own eye will tell you that a short round posy in the top of a tall thin vase looks as ridiculous as the decidedly top-heavy arrangement on the right.

over method is probably the simplest to do if you are a beginner and it is the way you would work to make a sphere, or a cone, or a "picture frame", for example.

Setting the height and width of an arrangement is something that quickly comes with experience, the governing factors usually being the size and shape of container, the sort of flowers you are using, and the space you have to put the container in. As a rough guide, an arrangement never looks happy if the flowers are very much shorter than the container, and they start to look top-heavy if they are more than twice the height of the container below them. The width can be more flexible, but always aim for generosity rather than skimpiness because a cramped arrangement looks fussy and rather mean. Having said this though, once you have greater confidence there is no reason why you shouldn't make arrangements to any proportion you choose and be successful. They may look fine to someone else, but if you aren't satisfied you can always split them up and start again. Just aim to be as relaxed as you can and as flexible as possible, and then your creativity will have a good chance to develop.

1 *Select your basket for the fireplace arrangement, then wire the correct sized foam in place – front to back. Tie back the handle out of the way, but it will be useful later for handling the arrangement.*

2 *Build up the outline shape of the whole arrangement: Limonium, Poppy heads and grasses each add to the overall profile.*

3 *Once the framework is shaped, add the flowers keeping the colours bunched together and adding the dark colours last.*

Far right *The symmetrical shape, and the width and depth at the base of this arrangement perfectly complements the chunky squareness of the stove. And the colours, grouped for best effect, stand up well against their sombre backdrop.*

Special Arrangements

Dried flowers don't have to be arranged in containers of course. There are endless other ways of using them: on a base of foam cut to any shape you choose; or wired onto ropes and garlands, or made into tiny posies or into large sheaves. They can be a very useful decorating device, but remember they will not last for years and years.

Sheaves

One of the prettiest and simplest ways of showing them off is based on the look you get when hanging bunches to dry. Choose flowers, foliage and seed heads with good long stalks and simply lay them out together to make a well balanced bunch. If you want to hang the finished bouquet against a wall or piece of furniture, do this on a flat surface so that the best blooms are facing the front. If any stems aren't long enough to reach the end of the bunch, simply wire them to one of the longer pieces. Finally, wire all the stems together and cover this with a bow made from ribbon or a soft swathe of furnishing fabric, or simply wrap over the wire with a handful of soft grasses or other flexible material. A small wire loop can be attached to the back of the wire fastening so that the sheaf can be hung on a pin fixed to the wall. This type of arrangement looks particularly pretty when it contains lots of grasses and grains such as wheat and simple unsophisticated flowers, like a harvest decoration. If you like, you can add extra decoration with small fabric bows wired into the flowers. Pink the fabric edges for a special effect but keep it simple, and don't be tempted to add too much and detract from the flowers.

The sheaf idea can be elaborated to make long swags running the height of a wall or piece of furniture such as a dresser, or it can be adapted to make tiny bunches that are useful for attach-

ing to furnishings or corners of furniture or picture frames. Sheer fabric curtains caught back with a bunch of dried flowers at a window or a four-poster bed would look charming; or a group of tiny bunches at the top corner of a china display cabinet might echo the colours and designs inside the cupboard.

Foam bases

The method of packing flowers tightly together on a foam base to create a thick surface of texture and colour can be used on many different shapes. Large room decorations to hang for example, above a door or window frame, are best made by this method, but they will need a foundation for the foam to be fixed to.

Wooden battens or a plywood base must be cut into the rough shape of the finished arrangement and plenty of nails knocked through from the back to hold the foam in place. Fix rings or loops at strategic places along the top edge to hang the final thing over picture hooks on the wall. It would be difficult to work with an arrangement in situ high up above a window for example, so hang it at just above eye level.

Above *A simple, loose sheaf. The emphasis on a single colour and the free informality of the longer flowers gives a "country" flavour.*

1 *To make a more structured sheaf – here a predominantly white and yellow scheme – collect, ready for use, your implements and flowers. Loosely wire and fan out your longer stemmed Gypsophila and Larkspur.*

2 *Build up the sheaf carefully; hold the stems in one hand, while positioning the flowers and then wiring them in with the other. Group the variations of flowers for better contrast and profile.*

3 *To achieve a good finish with the shortest stemmed varieties, wire up two little posies separately and then wire them with stems crossed to the stems of the main sheaf.*

4 *Cover all the messy wire with a silk ribbon or some very light fabric in a complementary colour, but leave a loop of wire protruding at the back to hang the sheaf up with.*

Pyramids, balls, trees, wreaths . . .

All these shapes are based on the method described above and rely on a foam foundation on which to build up the flower arrangement. Pyramids and cones are popular for formal designs for either a table decoration or mantelpiece, but they can look very predictable if the flowers aren't chosen with care. A ring or wreath shape either to lay flat on a table or to hang vertically against a wall needs a circle of foam and a thickness deep enough to hold the short stems securely.

Other shapes, such as hearts or bows, are all possible, depending on your skill at carving and cutting out the foam base. All these methods are a marvellous way of using up flowers with very short stems or tiny bits left over from larger arrangements.

Mop head trees

This idea translates happily from the tiniest miniature version to a large and very grand floor-standing tree. Whatever size you choose, be sure that the base is good and heavy because the centre of gravity of these trees is high and the whole thing is prone to topple over. A clay garden plant pot makes a perfect container, whether or not you finally stand it in something more decorative later. If you know that it will be covered, then an old tin can, worn-out bucket or plastic box will be quite suitable.

Clay is ideal if you use cement to fix

To make a mop head tree you will need: Bonding cement, base container, pre-formed foam ball, a stick – cut to size – for the trunk and pebbles or similar for the base and selected flowers with stems cut to length such as those illustrated.

the stem in place because the two materials bond together as they dry. This is not the case with other materials, but it doesn't matter because the weight inside the container holds it all in place anyway.

Choose the base container and a pole or trunk of some kind. A straight, smooth, symmetrical pole will give one sort of effect, while a rough lichen-covered, natural branch, which is bent and wobbly, will obviously look quite different, so decide the style you are

aiming for. A plain pole can be wrapped with raffia, ribbon or fabric after the arrangement is finished or the wood can be stained, painted or lacquered *before* you begin. Stand the pole in the centre of the pot and anchor it temporarily with tape and sticks across the top. Plug the drainage hole with clay and then fill with plaster or cement. Once the base is firm, anchor a block of expanded foam to the top of the pole. You may need to join several pieces together with wire and tape if the tree is large. Wire netting wrapped around foam holds it in place round the pole, but as a precaution, tape around the pole under the foam to stop it slipping down with the weight of flowers. You do not need to cut the foam into a sphere because a rough cube will do, but for small trees you can buy ready-made spheres that make the job very easy to do.

The choice of flowers is up to you. You can mix varieties and colours, or use just one type of flower, which can look stunning. Tiny trees made simply from Lavender heads are very pretty, or a larger tree could be made from a cloud of Gypsophila for a very airy delicate effect. Reindeer moss and lichens have a wonderful earthy look, and seed heads used alone have a neat formality when massed in this way.

1 *Fill the base container up to three-quarters full with cement mixture and shove the "trunk" firmly right down in the centre, making sure that it is standing in a true vertical.*

2 *Dig a hole in the foam ball with a sharp knife, fill it with cement, and press it firmly on to the top of the "trunk". Clean off the excess cement with a knife.*

3 *Press a few decorative pebbles or shells into the cement. This will support the base of the trunk and help counterbalance the mop head. Put aside for at least 24 hours to set hard.*

4 *Start off the mop head with your selected space filler such as Limonium and then establish the outer limits of the profile with such materials as longer stemmed Poppy heads and grasses.*

5 *The mop is now built up with the rest of the selected flowers. It is worth remembering that mop head trees, whatever their size, are most effective when they are densely filled and achieve real symmetry.*

6 *The mop is now finished, but you can add a few last touches before you put the tree in its final position, such as Hydrangea petals, cemented or glued on to the pebbles which give a nice effect of fallen leaves.*

Posies

Round posies have a lovely old-fashioned feel to them and make superb presents. Several together can stand in a container to make an instant arrangement and a pair in tall candlesticks look pretty as a table decoration. For these posies use flowers and other materials of roughly equal size of head. Start making the posy from the centre flower, which should be something solid and pretty, such as a rosebud. Add flowers from the centre outwards, either at random or in concentric rings. The rings can be all one colour or mixed. A little mixed bunch looks fresh and pretty, while a posy worked in coloured rings looks more formal, like a Victorian brides-maid's bouquet. The final row looks best finished off with leaves as you would a fresh posy, and a lacy paper frill is easily added, made from a doiley taped or wired round the stem. The stems may need covering with thin tape or ribbon to make them comfortable to handle. Trim off the bottoms of the stems level to give a reasonable length of handle, bind them, then finish off with a bow tied up under the flowers, or make a loop so that the posy can be hung up somewhere. Posies are particularly attractive if scented flowers and leaves are incorporated such as a row of Lavender, Rosemary or Roses. It is instinctive to smell them so try adding scent, this action is always well rewarded.

Picture and mirror frames

Using either the technique of covering areas of foam with small flowers, or using tiny bunches, you can transform a frame for pictures, photographs or mirrors.

If it is to be temporary, then you will have to avoid glue and nails but you can still wire little clusters of flowers into the corners or all along one or more edges.

A large wooden frame can be covered with foam if you don't mind its being a permanent arrangement. This works best on a big frame because the depth of foam needed to hold flowers will look odd and out of scale on anything very small.

Another method is to twine flexible stems or those inclined to twist, such as Hops, into the shape of the frame and then wire the small flowers to this base. The circlet of flowers can then be fixed to the frame with a tiny piece of double-sided tape or thin wire if it can be hidden.

Ropes and garlands

You can use dried flowers to make ropes and garlands, to drape or twist down stairs or across walls, or for special occasion effects such as at Christmas time. Even when in place these arrangements are fairly fragile so need to be kept out of reach of children if possible,

Above *Tiny posies make pretty presents to give away and, dropped into a small cup or vase, make an instant arrangement. Pale creamy Helichrysums are thrown into relief by a lacy backing that is the key to the success of the posy.*

Right *A woven table mat frames and finishes a pretty mixture of Roses, Helichrysums, Sea Lavender, Statice and Poppy heads. The flowers are built up onto a shallow disc of florists' foam fixed to the mat.*

otherwise the temptation to swing on them might prove too much.

You will need a soft rope that curves well into shape and which is an unobtrusive and natural colour. Boat chandlers are the best source for this. You then need to make tiny groups or bunches of selected flowers and wire them onto the rope, the idea being to cover as much as possible of the rope's surface. This may be easier to do in situ because the back of the rope need not then be so carefully covered. It is slow work and time-consuming, so don't be too ambitious and don't expect to make miles of garland at one time.

Above *The lightest most ethereal wreath made from a twist of Honesty seed pods and Forget-me-not seed heads.*

Top right *A country posy of mixed colours and flower types made to be viewed from any direction and best displayed on a low piece of furniture.*

Bottom right *A solid and fairly formal wreath made using a foam base. This is packed with Sea Lavender and then studded with highlights of yellow and cream flower heads. It can be hung on a wall or would make a perfect table centre. Leave it entirely plain or add a matching bow for frivolity.*

CULTIVATION

The success or failure of growing plants for drying will depend on two things – the vagaries of nature: gales, floods, droughts, frosts, invading armies of pests and epidemics of disease all bent on devasting your precious plants, and on *you*. The understanding of what your own garden requires to encourage the healthy plant growth of all sorts of varieties each with their own special needs, is the basis of any gardener's success. Here, we have summarized the essential gardening know-how for working *with* nature to grow to perfection what you want, where you want.

Weather and Climate

The climate in a garden depends first upon major factors, such as latitude, distance from the sea and prevailing winds, and secondly on the local topography. The local climate can vary quite considerably from place to place even in a very small area.

Plants that will grow in a given climate are said to be hardy in that area. Hardiness depends upon resistance to frost and upon adaptation to the cycle of seasons prevailing. Thus, plants hardy in sub-tropical areas are not hardy, and must be given protection, in more northern zones. Conversely, sub-arctic plants used to short growing seasons and long periods of dormancy may not thrive in temperate places.

The aspect of a garden will influence greatly the types of plant that can be grown. In the northern hemisphere a south-facing slope will receive the maximum amount of light and heat because the ground is presented to the sun at a direct angle. Growth will start earlier in the spring and continue until later in the autumn. Flat ground, or land sloping in directions other than south, is presented to the sun at a more acute angle and therefore the light and heat it receives are less intense and spread over a shorter part of the year. Light is naturally less intense during the winter when the sun is lower in the sky, and sites that are reasonably well lit in the summer may be shady right through the winter. Ground overshadowed by trees and buildings will be cooler and less hospitable to plants requiring good light, but it will provide an ideal situation for plants native to woodlands. Walls facing north receive less light than south-facing walls, while east- and west-facing walls get full sun for about half the day.

During the day the soil absorbs sun heat and then, under normal conditions, gives off this heat at night when the air above it cools, In this way the soil acts as a heat store, and the heat it radiates protects the plants above it from frost. However, if the soil is mulched it cannot absorb heat so effectively during the day and therefore has less to give off at night. For this reason mulches are laid on the soil in spring and dug in during autumn to allow the soil to absorb more heat in winter. Weeds prevent the absorption of heat in the same way as a mulch and so should be kept under control at all times.

Soils vary in the rate they give off heat absorbed during the day. Clay soils are slow to warm up, and also store heat for longer. Sandy soils absorb and give off heat quickly. Compacted ground is a more effective radiator of heat than soil that has a finely-tilled surface. This acts as a blanket, keeping in the heat and allowing the plants above to become frosted. Walls absorb and give off heat in the same way as soil, which is why tender plants thrive when grown against them.

Wind can be a destructive force and the strong winds of exposed places cause much damage to foliage of both woody and herbaceous plants. Wind force can be much reduced by planting hedges or constructing screens as so-called "wind breaks". Solid walls or fences are not desirable because these merely divert the wind and do not reduce its force. But a permeable barrier such as a planted coniferous, evergreen or semi-deciduous hedge can effectively reduce wind speed for a distance up to ten times its own height.

Many species of plants used for the production of flowers or foliage for drying and preservation are half-hardy. It follows that they respond significantly by increased production of quality material when grown in well chosen or created sheltered positions.

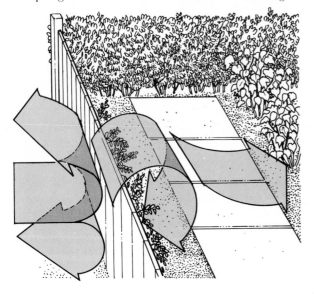

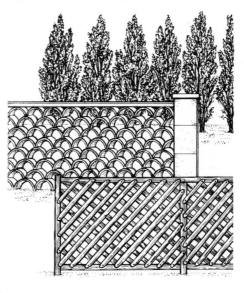

Solid windbreaks (far left) *create turbulence that will damage plants close to them. More open screens such as sturdy trellis, of wood or preformed concrete, or open hedging* (near left) *are best.*

Soil

Soil profiles tend to vary from area to area, depending upon geology, climate, the history of cultivation and the vegetation cover.

Types of soils
From the gardener's point of view, soils are classified according to the amount of sand or clay particles they contain, and according to their acidity or alkalinity.

Clay soils are usually rich in nutrients, but are heavy to cultivate and warm up slowly in the spring. The addition of organic matter greatly improves clay soils because it causes the particles to clump together in larger groups, so allowing water and air to pass between them. Lime, when added to clay soils, also causes particles to bind together.

Sandy soils are easy to cultivate and quick to warm up in spring, but they dry out very easily and, because of their rapid drainage, nutrients are quickly washed away. Sandy soils may be improved by adding organic matter such as garden compost.

Silty soils have particles intermediate in size between sand and clay. The texture of silt soils is improved by applying large amounts of humus-producing material.

Loam is the ideal soil, containing a mixture of clay and sand, or silt particles, plus an adequate supply of organic matter and plant nutrients. It is easy to cultivate, retains moisture and nutrients, yet is well-drained. Loam varies between light, medium or heavy, depending on the clay-to-sand ratio.

Peat Made up of partially decomposed organic matter, peaty soils are inclined to be acid and poorly drained. The addition of lime nutrients, coarse sand, grit or weathered ashes, and the con-struction of artificial drainage systems improves their quality.

Acid and alkaline
A soil rich in lime or chalk is said to be alkaline. One that lacks lime is described as acid or sour. The degree of acidity or alkalinity is measured on the pH scale, which runs from 0 to 14. A soil with a pH above 7·0 is alkaline, and one with a pH of below 6·5 is acid. Most plants prefer a soil with a pH in the range 6·5 to 7·0.

Humus
The dark brown, crumbly organic matter within the soil is humus. It consists of plant and animal remains in various stages of decay and ensures the continued survival of bacteria, which are essential if a soil is to be fertile. Humus also retains moisture, keeps the soil well aerated, and is a source of plant nutrients. On cultivated ground humus breaks down more quickly than it would if left undisturbed, so it is important that the soil is amply replenished with well-rotted manure, compost, leaf-mould or other humus-forming material whenever possible.

Soil Life
Earthworms, insects, burrowing animals, slugs, snails, bacteria and many other forms of life all contribute to the organic content of the soil and, except for those that are a severe nuisance, they should be encouraged.

Drainage
Both water and air are necessary in the soil if plants and soil organisms are to thrive. In poorly drained soils, the roots of plants are restricted to the top few inches of ground where they cannot anchor the plant firmly or search very far for nutrients. Lack of air inhibits the uptake of minerals from the soil.

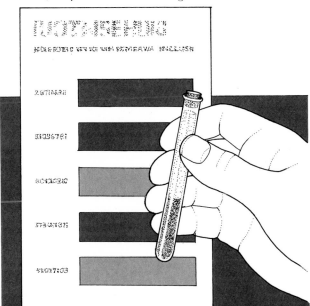

Simple soil testing kits are available for testing the soil's pH level, which should be done fairly regularly if you are attempting to modify the pH level of your soil.

Improving the soil

Humus is an essential constituent of good soil. In dry soils it acts as a sponge, helping to retain water and the plant food in nutrient form which is dissolved in that water. In wet soils and especially in clay, humus is essential as an aid to drainage and aeration.

Most plants thrive in soil that has been dressed with well-rotted manure or compost in the autumn before planting. Fresh manure should not be added to the soil before it has had a chance to decay, because in its fresh state it gives off harmful ammonia.

A very wide variety of organic materials are used to improve soils and any of the following are suitable.

Leaf mould – Decayed leaves of deciduous trees collected and composted in autumn.

Animal manures – Animal faeces usually mixed with some form of bedding such as straw, peat, wood shavings or sawdust. Manure is best used when well rotted, which means that it should be stacked and allowed to decompose before being added to the soil.

Peat – Partially decayed plant matter usually obtained from bogs or wetlands. This is an ideal material.

Garden compost – The product of properly prepared compost heaps is an ideal humus forming additive for all soils.

Spent hops – The organic by-product of brewing, usually obtainable as a dried material often with inorganic fertilizer additives.

Sawdust – This material does not decay rapidly, tends to acidify soil, and is difficult to compost. It is, however, very valuable when used as a mulch.

Spent mushroom compost – These composts can have an exceptionally high nutrient content. Unfortunately they often also contain calcium in a chemical form which is not much used in agriculture. Care should therefore be taken, and before using this material in large quantities it would be advisable to have a sample analysed, and afterwards advice about amounts that can be used safely.

Seaweed – Gardeners in coastal regions can collect this material, which can be composted to create an excellent organic manure.

Pulverized bark – A most valuable material for use mainly as a soil surface mulch. Very slow in breaking down.

Sewage sludge – Dried sludge contains a good deal of nitrogen but is not high in organic content. It is best used as a material for incorporating into a soil during the autumn cultivation operations.

Green manure – The growing of a crop for the purpose of digging it into the soil as a humus-forming material is common practice in arid areas.

Inorganic soil conditioners
On heavy soils the incorporation of inorganic soil conditioners such as weathered wood and fuel ashes, coarse sand and grit, may be of considerable help in making cultivation easier. These materials will open up the soil to some degree, allowing in air but are best applied in combination with organic matter rather than on their own.

Modifying pH
Ground limestone will improve the structure of a clay soil, but it is as a means of adjusting the acidity, or sourness, of a soil that it is of greatest value, especially on light, sandy soils which lose lime rapidly by leaching. Some bacteria also will not thrive in acid soils and liming improves the breaking down of organic material.

Some plants find it easier to extract nutrients from an acid soil, others prefer to grow on limed soil. While it is generally advisable to grow plants that are suitable to the soil, sometimes this is neither desirable nor practicable. Then the pH, or acid/alkali balance of the soil

has to be adjusted.

A soil with a pH of between 6·5 and 7·0, or neutral, will grow a wide range of crops, and 6·8 is the figure to aim for when correcting acidity. Soil with a pH balance below 6·5 affects the uptake of major and minor plant nutrients. Hydrated lime (calcium hydroxide) is the most effective type to use for pH adjustment because relatively small amounts of it will be needed. It is also more stable than the more expensive quicklime. Ordinary ground limestone or chalk (calcium carbonate), often cheaper, can be used. An advantage is that it can be used just before planting or sowing without damage to the crop.

More lime will have to be applied to acid clay soils, and those containing large quantities of organic matter, than to acid sandy soils. Acid soils should be tested annually and suitable amounts of lime added to replace that lost by the soil in the previous season.

Applications of lime are usually made in autumn or early winter. Lime should not be allowed to come into contact with manure or it will react with it, releasing valuable nitrogen into the air. Apply lime and manure in different years, or allow several weeks to elapse between the digging in of the manure and the dusting of the lime. Left on the surface of the soil the lime will gradually be washed in. If necessary, a vegetable plot may be limed in autumn and manured in winter with no ill effects.

Alkaline soils
It is much more difficult to alter the pH of an alkaline soil than that of an acid one. Start by enriching the soil with peat and other acidic organic matter, which will lower the alkalinity to some degree. Then apply flowers of sulphur at the rate of 115g per m² (4oz per yd²) on sandy soils and 230g per m² (8oz per yd²) on heavy soils. Test the soil at monthly intervals to monitor the pH. At below pH 6·5 the availability of nitrogen, phosphorus, potassium and molybdenum decreases while that of iron and manganese increases. On soils with a high pH, calcium decreases the uptake of potassium. If the soil is very alkaline, apply flowers of sulphur each year, but also try to grow plants that will tolerate some degree of alkalinity. An efficient drainage system will help to leach some of the chalk out of the soil.

Where iron deficiency is a problem on chalky soils, iron chelates or sequestrene can be watered on to make this nutrient more readily available. Three or four applications a year at the manufacturer's recommended rate should be sufficient for most gardens.

Fertilizers such as sulphate of ammonia are acid-reacting and should be used on chalky ground in preference to fertilizers of an alkaline nature.

Types of fertilizers

There are two basic kinds of fertilizers: organic and inorganic, and both are valuable in the garden.

All organic fertilizers contain carbon and have been derived from living organisms. Before organic fertilizers can be absorbed by the plant they must be broken down in the soil by bacteria and fungi into inorganic chemicals. It will be seen from this that organic fertilizers actually encourage soil bacteria and so increase fertility. They are released for plant use relatively slowly.

Inorganic fertilizers do not contain carbon. They cannot improve soil texture and do not add any humus, but they are often quick-acting and, by weight, richer in nutrients and are cheaper than organic fertilizers.

The conscientious gardener will use a combination of organic and inorganic fertilizers together with bulky organic soil conditioners to improve his land and keep it in good condition.

All fertilizers are labelled to show their nutrient content in terms of nitrogen (N), phosphoric acid (P_2O_5) and potash (K_2O). Some fertilizers are described as "straight", meaning that they supply just one of these nutrients; others are called "compound" and supply varying quantities of all three nutrients.

Application

Fertilizers may be applied to the ground before sowing or planting (in which case they are known as base dressings) or while plants are growing, as top dressings.

Apply base dressings to the soil a few days before sowing or at the time of planting, working the fertilizer into the top few inches of soil with a fork or rake.

Dust top dressings of fertilizers around growing plants while the soil is moist and hoe them lightly into the top few inches.

Certain fertilizers are sold in soluble powder or liquid form and can be watered onto the soil or sprayed over plant foliage. These foliar feeds are generally quick-acting and should be applied when the soil is moist. Foliar feeds are best given in dull weather rather than in bright sunshine.

Assessing plant needs for nutrients

Most plants grown to produce a crop of flowers or foliage for drying or preserving will be adequately supplied with nutrients if given a base dressing of a compound fertilizer before being sown or planted. Exceptionally some of the perennials such as Delphinium and Achillea will require one or even two top dressings of inorganic fertilizer lightly hoed into the soil around them during the growing season. The perennials and shrubs referred to in this book would all benefit from annual mulches of compost or manure applied around their root zones in late autumn or winter.

Animal manure may be difficult to obtain, and proprietary organic soil conditioners are expensive. An alternative source of bulky organic matter is garden compost. A compost heap will cheaply and quickly turn garden and kitchen waste into valuable soil-enriching material.

Principles of compost-making

To make good, crumbly compost the heap must be properly constructed so that the organic material can decompose rapidly and not turn into a pile of stagnant vegetation.

Air, moisture and nitrogen are all necessary if bacteria and fungi are to break down the raw material efficiently. Air is allowed in through the base and sides of the heap. Water should be applied with a can or hose if the heap shows signs of drying out, and moisture can be kept in by covering the heap with burlap, old carpet or polyethylene sheeting. Nitrogen in the form of manure, compost activator or a nitrogenous fertilizer will aid bacteria and fungi in the breaking-down process.

The heap will be able to function best if it is sited in a sheltered and shady place but not under trees or where tree roots may move into the compost. It must be protected from becoming dried out by the sun and wind.

Organic materials are best dug in: in dry soils they help to retain moisture, in clay soils they aid aeration and drainage.

1 Choose a suitable site for the heap, and then erect the sides with wire or wooden slats. A slatted wooden floor is optional.

2 Scatter a nitrogenous fertilizer over the first layer of compostable material to encourage decomposition.

3 Add further layers of compost material and nitrogenous fertilizer, water if looking dry and keep the heap covered.

Compost heaps made in spring will produce valuable soil-enriching material ready for use by autumn. Heaps made in autumn and winter need longer to decompose and the material will not be ready for use until the following summer.

Compost bins

It is possible to rot down compost satisfactorily by simply stacking it in a spare corner of the garden, but in this way the heap may become untidy and the material on the outside will dry out. Decomposition will take place more rapidly in a home-made or proprietary compost bin that allows air in and retains moisture. For best results, compost bins should not be more than 1·5m (4ft) high, and they can be much longer than wide.

There are many ways of making a compost bin. One of the simplest is to erect a square or oblong cage of wire netting, supported by four stout posts driven into the ground. Make the front removable to allow access to the rotted compost. It is advisable to construct a false floor in larger bins – the easiest method being the use of planks supported on bricks with small gaps to allow for air penetration. Disused fork-lift pallets are ideal for the purpose, and line the inside of the cage with newspaper to prevent excessive drying out. A

piece of burlap or polyethylene can be weighted down with bricks on the top of the heap to keep the moisture in.

A more solid structure can be made from angle-iron posts and wooden boards fashioned with gaps to allow in a certain amount of air. The internal structure of the heap is the same as for a wire cage. Brick or concrete block structures may be used provided that occasional vertical joints are left unmortared to allow in air. The fronts can be equipped with removable wooden slats.

A series of two or three compost bins is very useful. When one bin is full the compost can be left to decompose and another bin brought into use. In this way a cycle of compost production can be kept going.

There are many proprietary compost bins available but check that the bin is strong and large enough for your garden's compost needs, bearing in mind the length of time it takes to decompose.

Compostable materials

One of the secrets of ensuring rapid decomposition is not to allow large quantities of one particular material to build up in the heap. All the following materials may be composted if properly mixed together: annual weeds, grass clippings (unless the lawn has been treated with hormone weed killers),

potato peelings, tea leaves, crushed eggshells, animal manure and urine, torn-up newspapers (but not glossy magazines), soft hedge clippings, dead flowerheads, pea pods, vegetable leaves and stems, tree and shrub leaves. Do not use woody material or any vegetation which has been sprayed with herbicides or is affected by diseases and pest.

Constructing the heap

When the bin has been erected the composting can start in earnest. On top of the false floor, if used, place a 15–25cm (6–9in) layer of compost material and lightly firm it down with the head of a rake or the back of a fork. Scatter sulphate of ammonia, calcium ammonium nitrate or urea – all of which are nitrogenous fertilizers – over this layer at the rate of 15g to m² ($\frac{1}{2}$oz to 1yd²) and then add another layer of compost material.

(Calcium ammonium nitrate may be used as an activator without additional lime being needed.) Never add lime and fertilizers at the same time and never mix these chemicals. Alternatively, a proprietary compost activator or animal manure may be added between the layers of vegetation but manure should not be allowed to come in contact with the fertilizer or lime. If it does valuable nitrogen will be lost. Keep a cover on the growing heap, and water when it

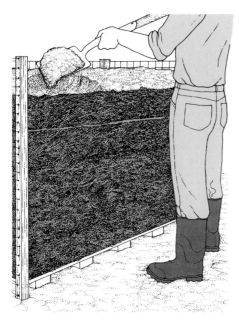

4 *When the bin is full remove the cover and finish off the last layer with a thin layer of soil.*

gets too dry. When the bin is full a thin layer of soil may be spread over the top instead of burlap or polyethylene.

Using the compost

In a well-made, sensibly filled bin the compost will not need turning, for virtually all the material will decompose sufficiently.

Check the heap at intervals and, if possible, shovel out the usable compost from the bottom. The compost should be brown and crumbly, although some of the material may still be recognizable. Unrotted material may be left behind as the basis of the new heap.

Use only very well-rotted compost as a mulch because partially decomposed material may contain active weed seeds that will soon germinate and become a nuisance. Alternatively, dig in the compost during soil cultivations in autumn and winter.

Leaf-mould

The leaves of deciduous trees and shrubs may be rotted down on their own to make soil-enriching leaf-mould. A wire bin (similar to that made for compost) makes a suitable container, and a suitable fertilizer can be sprinkled between the layers. A fast space-saving alternative is to pack the layers of leaves and fertilizer in black polyethylene sacks that have been perforated to allow in air, tied at the top and stood out of the way until the spring following autumn collection. Leaves in outdoor bins will take rather longer to decay. All leaves of deciduous trees and shrubs can be composted. Leaves of evergreens are not suitable. Leaf-mould can be dug into the soil or used as a mulch.

Leaves will rot down well in a perforated polyethylene sack tied at the top. The leaf mould will be ready to use the following spring.

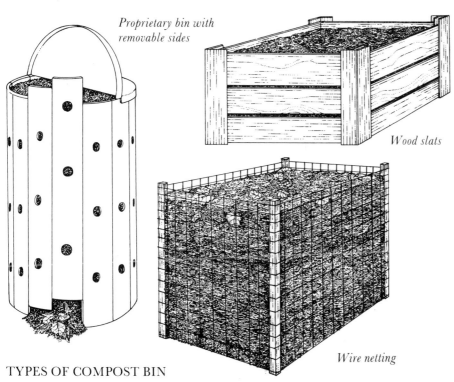

Proprietary bin with removable sides

Wood slats

Wire netting

TYPES OF COMPOST BIN

Watering

Plants will grow healthily without check, if they have constant access to water. In temperate climates, the soil normally contains sufficient moisture, but during very dry spells in spring and summer the plants may find it impossible to extract sufficient water to keep them turgid; they will wilt and growth will be temporarily halted. If not watered quickly, their leaves will turn crisp and brown and they will eventually die.

Plants being cultivated to produce flowers or foliage for drying or for preservation by other methods should be regarded as a crop; and to achieve maximum yields their growth should not be retarded for any reason.

Some of the plants grown for dried flower harvests are natives of drier areas of the world and in particular those species that have "everlasting" as part of their common name are indigenous to arid regions. Thus Anaphalis, Helichrysum, Helipterum, Phaenocoma and Xeranthemum all originate from areas of low rainfall and indeed grow best when grown in well drained, dry positions. Irrigation for these species is rarely needed. On the other hand, plants such as Dipsacus, Echinops and Typha, that are indigenous to wetter regions would most certainly need to be regularly watered.

As a general rule, 2·5cm (1in) of water will travel to a depth of 23cm (9in) in the soil. To water 0·5 hectares (1 acre) of land to this depth, a total of 102,966 litres (22,650 gallons) must be applied. Continuous, light applications of water during periods of prolonged drought are not to the plants' best advantage, and will only encourage the plants to produce surface roots, which will suffer in future droughts.

Sandy soils will dry out much more quickly than those containing clay, and will need to be watered sooner during spells of drought. The soil surface is seldom a good guide to moisture content, so dig down with a trowel to see if the soil below the surfae is moist. If it is dry or only just moist, water.

Water can be applied to the soil or to container-grown plants in several ways. On a small scale the watering can with a rose is a most useful device, but the labour-saving hose when the water may be sprayed, trickled, flooded or seeped onto the soil is often essential.

As a general rule it is advisable not to wet flowers as they can be damaged, and the more expensive trickle seep systems of irrigation are preferable.

General Cultivation Techniques

In warm protected areas half-hardy annuals can be sown where they are to flower – usually in rows but sometimes broadcast in beds. Sowing can take place once the ground has warmed – usually in late spring but in late years in early summer. Drills are taken out about 1–2cm ($\frac{1}{2}$–$\frac{3}{4}$in) deep. Seed is sprinkled very thinly along the drill and fine soil is pulled back to cover the seed. Some gardeners like to use so-called "marker plants" to indicate where the rows have been sown – radish which germinates rapidly can be sown exceptionally thinly with seed of the half-hardy annual flower. The seeds leaves of the radish quickly indicate the position of the row and allow hoeing or weeding to take place at an early stage. Annuals need to be thinned early in their lives so that those which are to be grown to maturity can have maximum light, space and supplies of plant food from the soil. When thinning, remove weak specimens first and leave the strongest plants. Two or even three thinning operations can be carried out leaving the selected specimen at the correct distance from its neighbours. Care should be taken to firm the seedlings to be retained because thinning in the row tends to loosen them in the soil.

In order to gain time or perhaps to ensure success in less protected areas, many gardeners use a greenhouse and/ or cold frames to raise their plants rather than risk sowing direct where plants are to bloom. The technique of raising seedlings of annuals for planting out can also be used for perennials such as Delphinium and Echinops.

Seeds of half-hardy and hardy annuals can be sown under cool glass in late spring. Perennials are usually sown in early summer.

Seed trays are filled with a suitable compost and the compost should be pressed lightly into the seed tray, which

Watering seedlings. *You should avoid sudden surges of water which can damage tender plants and displae compost. Start*

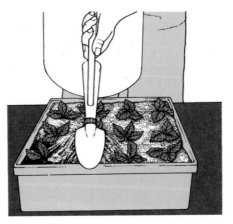

watering to one side of the tray or pot and then back and forth across before finishing clear of the container.

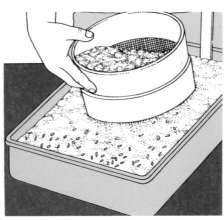

Sowing in containers **1** *Firm the compost to 1cm (½in) below the rim and scatter seed evenly over the surface.*

2 *Cover with a fine layer of compost, water, cover with a sheet of glass or paper and keep at recommended temperature.*

3 *After germination, remove glass and paper, keep the compost moist and spray with fungicide to prevent damping off.*

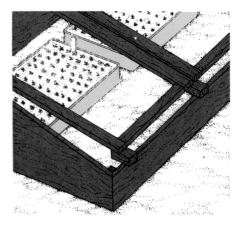

4 Pricking out. *As soon as they are large enough to handle, separate the seedlings carefully holding them by the leaves.*

5 *Make holes at the correct distance in hte compost; transplant seedlings, firming them in and water.*

6 Hardening off. *Place the plants in a garden frame or under cloches and increase ventilation until the covers can be removed.*

should then be watered with a fungicide. Seed is broadcast very thinly over the surface. To ensure even distribution very fine seed can be mixed with dry sand. The seed should be covered with up to 3cm (⅛in) of compost using a fine sieve to distribute this evenly. The boxes have to be watered using a can with a fine rose. It is usual to put a piece of glass over the boxes and shade them with newspaper until germination occurs. Alternatively, they may be put into a propagation frame that will provide the necessary warmth needed for germination. Once the first signs of germination are noted, the boxes should be given more light, but care must be taken to avoid strong sun, which would soon scorch the leaves of tender seedlings. Good greenhouse management is important at all times but during this critical stage it is particularly

important to ensure that boxes do not dry out, that the seedlings are allowed as much fresh air as possible, and that fungicide is used from time to time to prevent the so-called "damping off" organisms from attacking the tender young plantlets.

When the seedlings are sturdy and large enough to be handled, they should be pricked off into other seed trays or individually into pots. Plants for later planting out to produce harvests of dry flowers or foliage will certainly respond well when given individual treatment because later they can be moved to their growing positions in the garden with a minimum of root disturbance. During pricking out it is essential to avoid damage to the stem of the tiny plant, so handling by holding the leaves is advisable. Newly pricked out seedlings should be watered into their new situation

whether this is another seed tray or an individual container. A mild fungicide watering would be beneficial if disease is suspected. The seedlings are then grown on in a greenhouse or in a sheltered frame until ready for hardening off. For annuals this process of acclimatizing the seedlings to an outdoor atmosphere would usually take place from the end of spring. The seedlings are gradually exposed to more and more open air conditions so that they are toughened up and ready for planting out in their flowering rows or beds in the garden by the beginning of summer (hopefully when all danger of frost is over).

Perennial seedlings would also need to be hardened off, although these may well be grown on in larger individual containers until their final planting out time in autumn.

BIBLIOGRAPHY

Aas, K   *"Torking Av Blomster" (Drying Flowers)*
Norsk hagetid *91* (12) 386–388 (Dec 1975)

Azuma, S   "Acceleration of Flowering of *Statice* by Seed Ventilation"
J. Jap. Soc. Hort. Sci. *51* (4) (1983) 466–474

Bateson, N
De Yarburgh   *Dried Flowers – The Art of Preserving and Arranging*
Lutterworth (1979)

Baxendale, M   "Flowers for Drying"
Amateur Gardening Vol. 98 No 5103 p17 (1983)

Bolton, E N   *Dried Flowers with a Fresh Look*
Van Nostrand 1958

Bruenner, M   "Den Anbau von Trockenblumen planen" – The planning of dried
flower gardening. Gartenpraxis 1979 (1) 32–33

Condon, G   *The Complete Book of Flower Preservation*
Prentice Hall (1971)

Crater, D R   *The Dried Guide*
Tribune Publishing Co., Levington, NJ (1981)

Dolleman, E
& Van Dam   "Droogboeketten niet alleen met droobloemen"

Evans, D R   *Intensive Horticultural Crops* – No. 1 "Dried Flowers"
University of Bath (1981)

Fessler, A J   *Wertvolle Einjahresgrasser* – (Use grasses)
Gartenpraxis 1981 (3) 102–105

Floyd, G   *Plant it Now, Dry it Later*
McGraw Hill (1973)

Foster, M   *Flower Preserving for Beginners*
Pelham Books (1977).
Preserved Flowers – Practical Methods and Creative Uses
Transatlantic (1974)

Gordon, L &
Lorimer, J   *The Complete Guide to Drying and Preserving Flowers*
Webb & Bower (1982)

Joll, E   *Dried Flowers – Arrangements in Miniature*
Lutterworth (1976)

Karel, L   *Dried Flowers from Antiquity to Present – A History and Practical Guide*
Scarecrow (1973)

Kher, M A &
Bhutani, J C   Extension Bull. No. 2 Economic Bot. Information Service, Nat. Bot.
Res. Instit.
Lucknow, India (1979)

Knap, A   "Drying Flowers"
Ministry of Agriculture & Food, Ontario

Kreyger, J   "Equipment of Importance for Seed Drying in Europe" proc. Int.
Seed Test Ass. 28 (4) (1963)

Macqueen, S   *Encyclopedia of Flower Arranging*
Faber & Faber (1964)

Maltby F E   "Improved Methods for Preserving Botanical Specimens in Their
Natural Colours"
Museums J. *25* (12) (1926)

Matta, F B & Widmoyer, F B	"Production of Field Grown Statice *Limonium Sinatum* Mill. in the Espanola Valley, 1979" Res. Rept. Agr. Exptl. Sta. New Mexico State University (1980)
Matta, F B & Hooks, R F & Widmoyer, F B	"Field Production of Statice in the Espanola and Middle Rio Grande Valleys (1980)" Res. Rept. Agr. Exptl. St. New Mexico State University (1981) No. 459
Mierhof, A & den Boer & Vlamings, M	*The Dried Flower Book* RHS Enterprises (1982)
Morrison, W	"Preserving Plant Material with Glycerine" National Association of Flower Arrangement Societies of Great Britain. Leaflet No. 3. "Drying Plant Material" National Associaiton of Flower Arrangement Societies of Great Britain. Leaflet No. 4. "Preserving Flowers with Dessicants" National Association of Flower Arrangement Societies of Great Britain. Leaflet No. 8
Odell, O	*Dried Flowers* Hamlyn (1979)
Pierce, W D	"Retention of Plant Colours" Science *84* (2176) 253–4 (11 Sept 1936)
Rendle, A B	"Preservation of Natural Colour in Plants" Nature (9th Nov 1916)
Rothenburger, R R & Smith, J E	Drying Flowers and Foliage for Arrangements. Part of Subject Series "Grounds for Gardening" Univ. Missouri Extension Publications *221*
Rymer, G	"Drying Flowers (for dry arrangements) in a Microwave Oven" Amer. Hort. *56* (5) (Oct 1977)
Schofield, E K	"Botanical Crafts – An Annotated List of References" Plant Bibliography (Jan 1983) (4) New York Botanical Garden
Stevenson, V	*Dried Flowers for Decoration* Collingridge (1955)
Trail, J W H	"The Preservation of Green Colour in Botanical Specimens exposed to Light" Kew Bull. No. 2 49–52 (1908)
US Patents	3,979,837 – Ground rice hulls as a dessicant; 4,312,134 – Freeze drying
Wallis, L W	"Dried Flowers and Grasses from Seed" MAAF 9 Feb 1976, ER Ornamentals Group, 23 (personal communication).
Westland, P & Critchley, P	*The Art of Dried and Pressed Flowers* Ward Lock (1974)
Williams, F R	"Drying Flowers in Three Dimensions" Herbertia *9* 37–39 (1942). "Drying Plants in Three Dimensions" J New York Bot. Gdn. *44* (522) 138–141 (1943). "Flowers Dried in Borax: Notes After 8 Years of Experience" J New York Bot. Gdn. *49* (587) 251–253 (1948). Dutch Firms Concerned with Dried Flower Production Flower Trades Journal (Aug 1983) p.14. "To Preserve Autumn Foliage" Gardeners' Chronicle 11 (Oct 1930) Dried Sand Treatment for Preserving Flowers Missouri Bot Gdn Bull *21* (7) 105–107 (1933). "Preserving Plants and Flowers" Pharm J (24 Sept 1927) p.328

INDEX

ACKNOWLEDGEMENTS

Cover: LINDA BURGESS
Back Cover: CHRIS WRIGHT

HEATHER ANGEL: 21R, 26R, 61R
AVOTAKKA/Camera Press Ltd: 84–5, 87T
GILLIAN BECKETT: 25L, 31R, 55R
PAT BRINDLEY: 25R, 32BR, 41L, 44R, 46L, 49LR, 50R
LINDA BURGESS: 37R, 64–5, 80–1, 84, 85, 86L, 87BL
DAVID CARTER: 24R, 40L, 45L, 63, 66T, B, 67, 70, 78L, 79R
ALAN CORMACK: 10R, 30L, 31L, 33L, 39L, R, 40R, 46R, 47L, 48R, 50L, 54L, 56R, 58L
SUSAN EGERTON-JONES: 79
FLOWER COUNCIL OF HOLLAND: 9, 10L, 11R, 12L, TR, 13R, 16R, 18L, 19, 22TL, 26TR, 33R
KELLY FLYNN: 20R, 79R, B
R & C FOORD: 48L
CAROLE HELLMAN: 23R
W. HOGEWONING BV: 12BR, 14R, 15, 17L, 21L, 22TR, B, 23L, 24L, 27L, 28R, BL, 34L, R, 35L, 36L, R, 39TL, 41R, 42L, R, 44L, 47R, 51L, R, 56L, 57L, R, 58R, 76–7, 97TR, BR

JAHRESZEIT ZEN-VERLAG/Camera Press Ltd: 89
S & O MATHEWS: 62/3, 66–7, 81, 83, 86R, 87BR, 88, 90, 91, 92, 93, 94, 95T, 96R, 98–9, 99
TANIA MIDGLEY: 14L, 16L, 18R, 20L, 29R, 37L, 38R, 45R
MB/RHS Lindley Library: Endpapers
CARL NORDIN/Camera Press Ltd: 3, 97L
CLAY PERRY: 8–9
DAVID RAE: 11TL, 13L, 25TL, 26B, 38L
THE HARRY SMITH HORTICULTURAL PHOTOGRAPHIC COLLECTION: 17R, 30R, 52, 53R, 54R, 59R, 60L, 61L
UNWINS SEEDS LIMITED: 11TR, 28TL
MICHAEL WARREN: 29L, 55L
WILDLIFE MATTERS: 35R, 53L, 59L
JULIE WILLIAMSON: 60R
CHRIS WRIGHT: 69, 96L

T = Top, B = Bottom, R = Right, L = Left

Acacia Armata.